"'Finally!' That was the single word I returned to over and over as I read this book. Finally! Finally, someone, in this case two someones—two women—both pastors no less (seriously?!)—have had the courage to write down candidly and creatively what young adults are about as they move through the world as spiritual beings coping daily with the demands of life and love and living while at the same time genuinely in search of something that is greater than themselves. These two writers, young adults themselves, speak with a genuine spirit of humility, authenticity, and courage. They speak about God, Jesus, the Holy Spirit, the Church, the world, their generation, and themselves in ways that are not preachy but rather open conversation, not simply for the sake of conversation, but ultimately for the sake of what truly matters in this world and beyond. They speak to their own generation and to others who have gone before them and are coming afterward. Ultimately, they speak the truth in love, and I am so grateful...finally!"

■ Rodger Nishioka, Columbia Theological Seminary,
   Decatur, Georgia

WHO'S GOT TIME?

WHO'S GOT **TIME?**

SPIRITUALITY FOR A BUSY GENERATION

AMY FETTERMAN

AND

TERI PETERSON

CHALICE
PRESS

ST. LOUIS, MISSOURI

Cover art: iStock
Cover design: Scribe, Inc.
Interior design: Crystal Devine

Visit www.chalicepress.com

10 9 8 7 6 5 4 3 2 1   13 14 15 16 17 18 19

Print: 9780827243057   EPUB: 9780827243064   EPDF: 9780827243071

Library of Congress Cataloging–in–Publication Data available upon request.

To Anna Carter Florence, who pretty much kicked us in the you-know-what about writing a book already. Thank you for your support and belief.

CONTENTS

ACKNOWLEDGMENTS

Many, many thanks to the Young Clergy Women Project, for reminding us we aren't the only ones, for supporting us, offering opportunities and great new friendships, and being all around fabulous.

We are grateful to all our family and friends, who put up with our dreaming, our constant talking about this book for three years, and then our procrastination-induced panic. You are all wonderful and we love you. The same goes for our tweeps and Facebook friends, who offered support, inspiration, and just the right word when we needed it. Amy would especially like to thank her husband Dave for (among other things) being cool with a bride who worked on a book during their honeymoon and for finding the perfect way to lovingly tell her to quit watching Hulu and go write.

To our churches—Covenant Presbyterian Church in Staunton, Virginia, the Ridgefield-Crystal Lake Presbyterian Church in Crystal Lake, Illinois, and the Presbyterian Church of Palatine, Illinois—you have supported us, nurtured us, allowed us to try out these things with you, and journeyed with us and our slightly-outside-the-box leadership for many years. We are grateful for you and the ministry you do, and that you have allowed us to do it with you.

Thanks to Beverly Riddell and Sharlene Wade who helped us find the right words for sensitive topics; to Beth Bohannon for teaching us to sing; to Sarah Metivier who speed-proofread in exchange for Indian food; to Aric Clark, Andy James and Patrick Marshall for sharing their superhuman editing skills; to Julia Seymour and Ash White who helped us form community; and to Cecily Weber, who read chapters along the way (and in the middle of the night, and at the last minute) making sure that we weren't talking crazy. And many thanks to all our friends who engaged in new-to-them spiritual practices and were honest about whether or not they were actually spiritual.

We couldn't have done this without our public libraries. Thanks to Staunton and Crystal Lake libraries for not minding when we put entire sections on hold and ordered dozens of interlibrary loans. And thanks to all of you who support public libraries too, so we could do this work!

And to those who make our houses home, and who help by sitting on our arms and keyboards: Anyanka, Hallie, Fellini, Ollie, and Andrew. Yes, we can stop typing and pet you now.

FOREWORD

I wanted to make some connection with the small child, so I knelt down at his eye level and asked those obligatory grown-up questions. It's almost as if all people over the age of thirty-five have the same survey for children that we conduct, like official census takers. I found out how old he was, where he went to school, and what his favorite subject was. Then I asked, "What do you want to be when you grow up?"

He told me that he wanted to be an astronaut, and the announcement of his future occupation came with a stretch of his arms and some sound effects, as if he was intent on transforming into a rocket before my very eyes.

I nodded my head and smiled. I didn't dash his dreams. But honestly, I was thinking that the government has been cutting down on (wo)manned space flights and closing space programs, little by little. Though the excitement of exploration still lives in the bones of small girls and boys, the country has lost the political thrill of putting a man on the moon or dreaming about a journey to Mars. The industry has been privatized so much that any flight would be reserved for billionaires.

But I withheld my doubts as he began jumping and reaching for the sky. Instead, I kept bobbing my head and saying, "You would make a fantastic astronaut!"

I often feel like that little boy when I imagine what I want to be when I grow up. I want to be a spiritual person—someone who is peaceful, loving, and compassionate. Someone who can purposefully enjoy one thing at a time. Someone who can stop long enough to hear God in the hum of the earth. Someone who can easily access the ancient wisdom of our texts. Someone with the patience for meditation. I want to wear loose-fitting, gauzy outfits and let my hair grow out to a natural frizz.

Instead I'm stuck being the woman in jeans and a T-shirt, banging her fist on the steering wheel when she gets caught in traffic. I lose my temper with my family when I'm cleaning before company comes. I remain distracted by consuming some sort of media or information, buzzing and blinking at me from a screen. I feel like I need to be working all the time, because the stress of losing my job, of not being able to work, feels unbearable.

I don't want to be that person; yet, it feels impossible in our distracted culture to be anything else. So much of the spiritual life seems reserved for a different era, a time when people weren't so intent on proving their productivity. Or it's meant for a different life phase, when people weren't so indebted and anxiety-ridden.

The goal of spirituality felt shrouded and separate—like a monk in his saffron robe, secluded on a mountain temple in Thailand. With that myth of spirituality so far away from my gritty imperfections, I knew that I might as well plan on being an astronaut. I could raise my hands and jump up and down. But it remained out of my reach.

I decided to put away my dream for a spiritual life. I tucked it in with my 401K. Maybe at retirement I would be able to have that luxury.

Enter Amy and Teri. These two women come dancing into the discussion, with box-kicking wisdom. They remind me that the spiritual life is not to be separated from the fiber of our lives, but woven into it. We don't enter into spirituality with mournful solemnity, but we grab it with the tenacious humor that an abundant life demands. These Reverends remind me to be spiritual where I am, with the time I have, among all my flaws, stresses, and grit.

In *Who's Got Time?* Amy Fetterman and Teri Peterson banish spiritual myths to the impossible island where they belong. Through their amusing wisdom, they explain how spirituality can be alive, embodied, and engaged. They don't ask us to join them on some holy mountain, separated from the world, but they bring lifegiving faith and practices to our hectic, fast-paced, overly scheduled, and impossible lives. They invite us into an adventure that will change us radically and drastically, as they make spirituality accessible for all of us.

CAROL HOWARD MERRITT

AN INVITATION
BETTER THINGS TO DO

*"Awake my soul, for you were made to meet
your maker."*
—MUMFORD AND SONS[1]

One glance at our calendars will confirm what we already know about ourselves—our lives are crazy-busy, often so packed we can't even imagine fitting in one more thing. There's always something else we are "supposed" to be doing, something else we "should" try to cram into the already packed schedule so we can be more well-rounded, more attractive to employers or to potential romantic partners, more prepared for whatever curveball life might throw next; but there's never time to fit in those extra things. Yet in the midst of all the coming and going, the learning and working and searching and socializing and trying to stay on top of world news, local issues, our jobs, our families and friends, volunteering, and whatever else we are "supposed" to be doing, many of us are hungry for spiritual nourishment—ravenous, even. It may not always look like spiritual hunger; maybe instead it manifests as a love of song lyrics that connect to something inside, a need for ways to talk with friends on a deeper level, a yearning to just get out of the house and go for a walk. We don't always know how to fit it in, or whether it fits in at all, but this spiritual hunger is still there. We may not be avid church-goers, but we have that need to connect, to be nurtured and nourished—a need

---

1. Mumford and Sons, *Awake My Soul,* Island Records, 2009, digital download.

we can't seem to meet with the usual chicken-soup books we've seen in the Christian Life or self-help sections of our local bookstores. Instead we find ourselves often surprised, overwhelmed, and even a little suspicious at the sheer number of books that promise us the kind of strongest-possible-ever relationship with God that also miraculously leads to a better life, all for a mere $9.99! There are lots of books and lots of blogs, but no one seems to be writing for us—whether you call us the GenX-Millennial bridge, the X and Y, Generation Debt or Generation Me or Mosaics or Busters or Googlers or, as they say in some church circles, "the Missing Generation."

> "Uh, you know, I meant to, and then I got really busy."
>
> —BUFFY, UPON BEING ASKED IF SHE HAD AC-CEPTED JESUS CHRIST AS HER PERSONAL SAVIOR.[2]

Sure, people talk about us—mostly lamenting that we don't seem interested in following the plan laid out by the people currently in charge of our churches and other institutions. We don't fit the mold, so we must be a lost cause. In fact, too many religious types have written us off. We're too self-absorbed, *they* say, too caught up in our busy schedules, too late in our religious formation yet too young to understand.

But that's not it. That's not it *at all!* We get that there is something greater than us out there. Among the generations, it's the young adults who are more likely to say they believe in that which cannot be explained.[3] We are twice as comfortable as our parents' generation with the idea that life, the universe, and everything are beyond explanation.[4] In our lexicon, mystery is not a bad word. In fact, sometimes the only thing we can say is, "it's a mystery." And while we're more comfortable not solving that mystery than the older generations, we still long to connect to it. The vast majority of us think our spiritual life is important and many of us find our interest in spirituality increasing over the years.[5] But you know what's missing? People reaching out to share with us the joy of God, at least in a way to which we can relate.

We get the need for searching. That need pulses beneath our skin day in and day out. We understand belief in something greater than ourselves and a lot of us do see that "something greater" in the story of a man named Jesus. But we don't connect to the story the way our parents and

2. "The Freshman," *Buffy the Vampire Slayer* (episode 57, season 4.1), originally aired October 5, 1999.
3. Christian Piatt and Amy Piatt, *MySpace to Sacred Space* (St. Louis: Chalice Press, 2007),19.
4. David Kinnaman and Gabe Lyons, *UnChristian* (Grand Rapids: Baker Books, 2007), 125.
5. Robert Wuthnow, *After the Baby Boomers: How Twenty- and Thirty-Somethings Are Shaping the Future of American Religion* (Princeton: Princeton University Press, 2007) 128.

grandparents did. The same-ol'-same-ol' does not meet our wonderings or our needs. We're a people of a different time, different culture, different generation. Just as in every generation, 20- and 30-somethings now are facing things the generations before them and behind them didn't and perhaps won't.

Unlike in our parents' generation, we didn't just grow *into* a world where people moved away from families and moved a lot; that's what we *grew up with*. As such, relationships are different for us than for even our coolest, Facebook-ing parents. We are good at staying in touch via social media and texting because we have to be. Our friends are scattered across the state, the country, the globe. Our best friend this year may not be our best friend in five years, not because of any falling out, but because one or both of us has moved. We aren't huge on joining life-long membership civic groups, but call us up one night for a Habitat for Humanity build that weekend and we are there. We may not become members of churches but we'll develop community at our local coffee shop or bar. We find and make friends—make community—in our own ways; ways that recognize our own impermanence.

Not only do we move around a lot (or at least live with the constant awareness that moving may be on the horizon), we live fully aware that we are not alone in this world. And we're not talking space aliens. Our t-shirts are made in places like Malaysia and Korea, our favorite restaurant is the Indian place down the street, our local supermarket is where we can not only buy all kinds of world foods but also overhear conversations in languages from all over the world. Globalization is a given for us—with all the good (diversity!) and bad (fear!) that comes with it.

We also know (and often struggle with) the fact that our lives aren't going to look like our parents'. And that's really hard. Sorry, the world tells us, you probably won't meet your spouse in college, or at least won't marry him or her right after graduation. Hate to tell you, but you may not be young enough to still play football with your kids when they're teens. You can't always get what you want, so you may have those 2.5 kids but not the spouse. Our later marriages and later babies—if we do the marriage and kid thing at all—mean our lives turn out differently from what many of us grew up expecting they would be. Can't just put all that household stuff you need on a wedding registry—you've got to buy your own pots and pans now!

Speaking of expectations, we're learning to deal with the fact that we're the first American generation in a long time that is expected to have a lower standard of living than the generation before us. We know we won't work for the same company for 40 years and retire with a good pension.

Not only will we go through several careers in our lifetime, but the job turnover for our generation is pretty quick and will likely continue to be.[6] Even though we have more people in our generation with higher education than in previous generations, we are significantly more likely to live in poverty than older adults.[7]

The world is so different than it was fifty, or twenty, or even ten years ago. Even those who are well past their 20s and 30s feel it. With the constant backdrop of war and a sagging economy, all of us are experiencing life differently than those who came before us. Our generation is not only those in our age cohort, it's also a descriptor of all of us living together in this time. Our common experience of rapid technological change, political and cultural divisiveness, and economic uncertainty bring us together in ways we could never have predicted. It is both an exciting and terrifying time to be alive, which makes our longing for spirituality all the more urgent—even as we understand less about how to fulfill that longing with our overburdened schedules.

In this wonderful and weary life, a connection with the divine comforts and challenges, empowers and enlivens, soothes and supports. But how do we find that connection?

When we hear about religion or "spiritual practice" we so often think of things that take hours of dedication. But who has an hour every morning and evening? And if we can't do it like that, are we just spiritual failures? The stereotypes of a deep spiritual life are hard to fit into a 21st century young adulthood, so many of us are settling for "none." We have more opportunities but fewer meaningful resources for building a spirit-centered life.

Since change and uncertainty really are the only constants we know, we long to connect to the mystery of the divine! And no wonder the words and ways meant for people of a completely different context don't always resonate with us. We need a vision for living out our faith that speaks to what's going on, not just what's done and gone.

That's what this book hopes to contribute.

In the pages that follow, we (your intrepid authors) hope to provide a vision of spirituality that our fellow young adults can identify with and be nurtured by. The word *spirituality* has gotten a lot of hype over the past couple of decades but hasn't picked up a precise definition along the

---

6. Even before the "Great Recession," the average employment period was only 2.7 years. Carol Howard Merritt, *Tribal Church* (Herndon, VA: Alban Institute, 2007), 57.

7. "For those aged twenty-five to thirty-four, the poverty rate is 15 percent, compared with 10 percent for older working adults." Anya Kamenetz, *Generation Debt* (New York: Riverhead Books. 2006), 6.

way. It's one of those words you can read and understand perfectly, until someone asks you to define it in your own words. "Um, spirituality? Uh, that's… well, you know… about God and connecting and stuff," you might respond, knowing full well your verbalization doesn't even come close to what you understand inside.[8] For the sake of this book, we'll offer a definition of spirituality borrowed from a wise friend who says "it's the whole human life in its efforts at being open to God."

If spirituality encompasses "the whole human life" as we propose, we wouldn't blame you if you are shaking your head right now. If we're suggesting that young adults can engage their whole lives in efforts to be open to God, then clearly we've already forgotten what we said in the first paragraph—we young adults are really, really busy. Even when we're not doing anything, somehow we still feel busy. Life is fast-paced and the hurriedness is never-ending. So when do we find time to engage our spiritual lives, let alone live our whole lives trying to be open to God?

> **Spirituality is not a checklist, it's a way of life.**

Spirituality is not about a list you can check off or one practice you can do; it's about a way of life. This way of life doesn't necessarily require putting more things into our already packed, too-short days, but it does require a shift in vision and understanding.

Engaging life spiritually is about adding the God-connected, divine-seeking self to your list of identities: friend, student, parent, partner, coworker, sibling, mystery-chaser.

We all know that this is easier said than done—shifting our vision of ourselves and the world is hard work. We also know that while it's extremely difficult to think our way into a new way of life, living ourselves into a new way of thinking/being is definitely a possibility. Here's where practices come in. Spiritual practices can help to nurture the soul and heart for service. They empower us to be the change we wish to see, to embody the God we long to serve, to be one with the mystery that is among us and beyond us. Spiritual practices also remind us that, well, we practice. Don't set unrealistic expectations for yourself: practice does not make perfect in this case. We never reach perfection, we're never done learning, we never finish nurturing the relationship between God and our own spirits. But we can—and do—become more familiar and comfortable living that part of our identity.

---

8. This example of the nebulous nature of a definition may in fact be from one of your authors' own life experience…

While we work toward shifting our identities to encompass this reality, remember this too: just as we seek out God, God seeks us. It does indeed take two to tango, and God can sashay with the best!

In this book, we offer you a selection of spiritual practices that we hope will resource and renew your efforts at being open to God. These practices are ones we believe may be especially meaningful to young adults, though they are by no means limited to that age group. We offer these practices after examining our own spiritual journeys, surveying young adults from around the country on theirs, and trying things with small groups. As we offer many different ideas and practices, we also offer full permission to leave some practices untried. Incorporate what speaks to you and leave behind what doesn't. If you start to sense some "practice-fatigue" it's okay to put the book down and come back another time. We know there's a lot here, and not everything will be for everyone or every time. Bite off small pieces, experiment, then try something else.

Within this book, you'll find some (perhaps familiar) classics like centering prayer and *Lectio Divina*. You may also find practices you had never thought of: developing rituals for job transfers or the importance of indulgence in your journey. Each chapter explores an aspect of life and offers some ways to engage that part of life through a spiritual lens. Some practices are concrete ideas that will fit right into a packed schedule, some are about shifting perspective on things we already do, still others will actually take a little bit of intentional time. At the end of each chapter we've offered one suggestion, separate from the rest of the ideas, that you can try out right away even if you haven't read the whole thing yet. We also offer some books that look at the chapter's topic in further depth, in case something strikes your fancy and you want to learn more.

You don't need to read the book in order; each chapter is designed to stand on its own. As good Reformed[9] theological types, we would encourage you to start with the chapter on sacred text (chapter 1), but you certainly are under no obligation to do so. We promise we won't call you up and check in on you after you've purchased/checked out/borrowed this book. You will also notice that we write very much from our perspective as Reformed Christians. Therefore, the God we strive to be open to is the

---

9. ~waving hands wildly~ *"umm, Amy and Teri, what's "Reformed" mean?"* "Excellent question, fabulous new friend! 'Reformed' is a descriptor given to the theological tradition that arose out of the Swiss Reformation—the one spearheaded by John Calvin, about 30 years after Martin Luther started arguing with the Roman Catholic church about a whole bunch of stuff. The biggest deal things in the Reformed Tradition include the idea that everyone can and should read their Scriptures for themselves, in their own language, and that the word of God is the foundation of everything else in life. That's why we Reformed types suggest starting with the sacred text chapter." *"Thanks Amy and Teri!"* "You're welcome!"

God revealed in the person of Jesus Christ through the Holy Spirit. Yet even if this is not your own perspective, we hope (and believe) that this book and its offerings may be of use and help to you.

As you read, you might notice that some practices are better suited for an individual while others would work best with a group. Don't let the individualized nature of reading a book stop you from engaging the group practices. Grab some friends, throw a dinner party, and try acting out scripture after a couple of glasses of wine! Have fun!

Convinced? If not, no worries. Put this book back down and head for the nearest cup of soup or coffee (both being quite good for the soul). But if you're nodding your head at all, identifying with either the experience of being a young adult or that need to connect to the divine in some new, fresh way: keep reading. We invite you to enter into the conversation with us.

ONE

~~~~~~~~~~

THERE'S A STORY

"But…" Harry raised his hand instinctively toward the light-ning scar. It did not seem to be there. "But I should have died—I didn't defend myself! I meant to let him kill me!"

"And that," said Dumbledore, "will, I think, have made all the difference."[1]

We never could understand those groups of Christians who were filled with vitriol against the Harry Potter series. For one thing, the books are awesome and everyone should read them. For another, they're blatant Christian allegory. J.K. Rowling didn't speak much on the Christian parallels (even when she was be-ing attacked for encouraging witchcraft by people who couldn't distinguish fantasy from reality) because she didn't want to spoil the direction of the series for those who hadn't already caught on. A story about a boy who's special, who fights an evil that wishes to put others down and subjugate the world, who finds strength in friendship and who ultimately (spoiler alert) sacrifices his own life for the sake of his world, and then comes back from the dead in triumph: how do Christians read that and not go, "that sounds familiar"?

Rowling is drawing on the sacred story of Jesus, and she's in good com-pany. The messiah figure gets reimagined as Aslan of C.S. Lewis' *Chron-icles of Narnia*, Frodo from Tolkien's *Lord of the Rings*, Jerry Siegel and Joe Shuster's Superman, Joss Whedon's Buffy, and even Steven Spielberg's

---

1. J.K. Rowling, *Harry Potter and the Deathly Hallows* (New York: Scholastic, 2007), 703.

E.T. Why does this story get retold and remade so many times and ways? Simple: it's a really good story.

The story of Jesus' life and ministry, combined with the mystery of his death and resurrection, has provided the powerful narrative foundation of many stories for the past two millennia. Jesus himself was shaped by the story of the Hebrew people from creation to kingdom to exile to looking forward for hope in the future. And of course he told stories all the time to get his message across—that's all parables are: stories. As our professional storytelling friends say, the story form is one of the oldest and best ways to communicate meaning.

We are drawn to sacred stories because they tell us about God *and* about ourselves—who we are and why we are here. When we engage the stories from our faith traditions, we discover what our ancestors in the faith had to say about the big questions of life. We also dare to believe we can see a glimpse of what God has to say about those questions. This is true of every tradition's sacred text. While we talk about the Bible, including both the Old and New Testaments, the practices and the ideas behind them apply to most scripture, whether you read the Quran, the Vedas, or the Torah. Because the text is sacred (and in our Reformed Christian tradition, because we believe the Holy Spirit is a part of our reading, interpreting, and understanding), when we read or hear the stories of our faith, we might be blessed with an "aha" moment, a moment where it feels as though the Holy One has reached out and whispered "psst, this part is for you." Suddenly, our life is woven into the narrative of God and God's people. The joys feel brighter and the sorrows are accompanied by a compassionate community, and because it's sacred, because the living God is at work through this tapestry of heroes and heroines, failures and triumphs, lessons and mysteries, there's always another thread we can follow. Any given story can speak to you in myriad ways, depending on where you are and how the Holy is reaching out to you.

The simplest way to engage the sacred stories is to read. Yup, read. But remember, while we said it was simple, it's certainly not easy. Let's be honest: as much as we love scripture (and we do; we're big Bible dorks), we get bored or distracted or even fall asleep while trying to read about all those things God told the Israelites via Moses. Sometimes it feels like we're reading a classic book that everyone says is good, and we know it probably *is* good, but the language and the pace and whatever else just makes us want to put it down and head for the nearest guilty pleasure. In many ways, our sacred scripture is a classic; but it is also more. *War and Peace*, *Moby Dick*, and *The Canterbury Tales* all have meaning to convey, just like the Bible (and all have made people fall asleep while trying to read them, just like the Bible). But such classics have not had hundreds of millions of people throughout time and across cultures coming to their pages seeking direction, understanding, and hope. We believe that while the Holy certainly can and does speak through secular material, there is something unique about our sacred texts. As such, the scriptures of our faith traditions deserve our attention and our open spirits, even if they can occasionally induce either yawns or horrified glares!

Part of the challenge in reading sacred texts is that they're usually so *long*. Many people think of the Bible as one book, but it's not; it's a library of books. You've got history, mythology, poetry, allegory, genealogy, wisdom sayings, letters, and gospels, plus rewrites and sequels. You have stories that have gone from oral tradition to written word, and many are words the authors wouldn't have expected to be read, let alone considered holy, thousands of years later. You have blood and guts, betrayal and heroics, politics and sex. You've got tragedy, and yes, even comedy.

The first step in reading the Bible is getting a translation that works for you. You may have grown up believing there's only one version of the Bible: that good ol' King James. The King James translation has some merit, but mostly because it sounds pretty and Shakespeare-esque. Most of us don't use *thees* and *thous* anymore, so reading stories from another time and culture in a version of our language we don't speak anymore seems to us to be more of a barrier than anything else. What translation do we recommend, then? It depends on what you're looking for.

The New Revised Standard Version, which is what we're using in this book, is your best basic translation. The translators tried to be faithful to the original Greek, Hebrew, and Aramaic while making some adjustments for a modern audience. This translation is also a good one to choose because you can get it in a few fantastic study editions. The Harper Collins, the New Interpreters', and the New Oxford study Bible all have great introductions to give you the context for each book, and commentaries for the text that help to clarify confusing bits. The newly translated Common English Bible is another great basic translation with a bit more of a modern spin than the NRSV. Other folks we know enjoy Today's New International Version, the New Jerusalem Bible, and the New American Bible, Revised Edition (lots of new in there!). If you're interested in paraphrases, check out *The Message* by Eugene Peterson. It's an easy read and sticks fairly close to the original meaning of the texts. If you're willing to go out even further, you can pick up *Word on the Street* by Rob Lacey. This paraphrase doesn't cover the whole Bible (Lacey skips over big chunks), and it definitely includes some artistic license in its interpretation. Still, it's a gorgeous piece of literature and makes the text come alive. If you do pick out a paraphrase, we also encourage you to have one of the basic translations nearby. Read a story in the standard translation and then in the paraphrase.

Got a translation you like? Excellent. Now get to reading. Look for the voice of God in the text. Maybe you've been reading the Bible for years. Maybe you have favorite stories from childhood you'll pick up and read every now and again. Maybe your familiarity with this **Get to reading!** sacred text goes no further than Googling John 3:16 after seeing it plastered on an NFL player's face or on the bumper of a car that just cut you off in traffic. Wherever you find yourself, from biblical neophyte to scholar, we hope the following offers some ways to enhance your reading.

You can do what Amy did as a kid, start at Genesis and read until you get tired, then pick up where you left off the next day. If you do decide to start at the beginning and work your way through until the end, be forewarned: parts of Exodus get really, really dull. So dull that Amy never quite made it past those sections and rather than skipping over to something more interesting, she went back to *In the beginning* and started the whole process over.

A friend of ours also tried to start at the beginning and work her way through, and got bored at that same section of Exodus. Instead of returning to the beginning, she skipped ahead, and then just skipped around until she found herself in the Psalms. She wanted to read the Bible "right" but wasn't sure if she was…and then she came to Psalm 139. Something about this psalm was right for her in that moment. She felt God's presence with her as she read, a presence so wonderful and powerful it moved her to tears. That was the only time she read scripture during that week, thanks to life's busyness and all, but she kept going back to that moment and that feeling during her hectic week. She knew peace and she knew God. Sounds to us like she got this reading the Bible thing "right" after all.

If you need something a little more disciplined than skipping around and a little less daunting than starting at the beginning and reading until the end, try picking a book of the Bible and reading a chapter a day. Just one chapter from one book. That way, when the boring parts get particularly dull, you know you've only got a little bit to read that day. There are also books and websites dedicated to dividing scripture into sections so you can read the whole bible in a year, three months, and even 30 days. If you'd like to read the entirety of the Bible, following a set guide would probably help your discipline.

Another great tool for becoming exposed to all the wonderful and (sometimes) weird things the Bible has to offer is the lectionary. *The what?* you ask. The lectionary is a listing of different scriptures that have been appointed for certain days. There's the Revised Common Lectionary, which many Protestant denominations follow. It sets a three-year cycle of scripture readings for each Sunday and festival day. Take it upon yourself to read the scripture appointed for each Sunday during the week, and over the course of three years, you'll be exposed to a great deal of the biblical text. You can also follow the daily lectionary, which is just what it sounds like: texts for each day. There's not one particular daily lectionary most denominations follow; pick one and just stick with it. Where do you find these lectionary lists? You can buy a lectionary book or calendar, or you can just do what we do—Google the word *lectionary*. Different options will pop up, and you can decide which you want to use. Some church or denomination websites also list the day's lectionary readings, often along with prayers or meditations to help you as you read.

While you're reading scripture, take note of particular verses that stand out to you. Ignore what librarians everywhere have told you, and go ahead and underline verses or passages that grab your attention (as long as you're using a Bible that belongs to you). You might even take to memorizing your favorite lines. Yes, that does seem a little old-school, even to us, but it also makes sense. Many of us have favorite song lyrics or movie quotes available for instant recall; why not favorite Bible verses? No, we are not advocating having different parts of scripture memorized so you can transform into a bible-quoting, holier-than-thou pain in the neck. Don't ever use sacred stories to put someone else down; use them to build yourself and your community up. Having a really crappy day, week, year? Maybe knowing by heart the words "weeping may linger for the night, but joy comes with the morning" (Ps. 30:5) will help you get through the tougher moments. Feeling like nothing you do is good enough and failure is your middle name? Call to mind the words of Paul: "I am convinced that neither death, nor life, nor angels, nor rulers, nor things present, nor things to come, nor powers, nor height, nor depth, nor anything else in all creation, will be able to separate us from the love of God in Christ Jesus our Lord" (Rom. 8:38–39). Okay, that one's kinda long, but it's also really good. We all need that reminder every now and again that nothing and no one can separate us from the love of God.

LEARNING HOW TO READ

Thanks to the massive amounts of homework and assigned reading most of us have been given over our school years, many of us have had to become masters of the art of speed reading: skim a section for its main ideas, and if anything looks particularly interesting or involved, spend time reading each word and sentence. Otherwise, just keep skimming while you absorb the main message/meaning of the piece. Sure, you miss out on clever turns of phrase and interesting tidbits, but you get the thing read in time to write your essay or pass the test. The trouble comes when we read our sacred stories the same way we learned how to read for school. Much meaning is found in those turns of phrase and tidbits. When we skim our scriptures, we may miss out on the conversation God is trying to have with us through the text.

We need to learn to read again if we're going to enjoy a sacred text to its fullest. It may take a little longer than skimming, but it's worth the investment. Enter *Lectio Divina*. While the four stages of this practice were formally written by John of the Cross in the 16th century, variations on divine or spiritual reading (which is what *Lectio Divina* means in Latin) have popped up in writings since the time of Origen in the 3rd century. In other words, this practice has been going on way longer than speed reading. The resurgence of its use today can probably be attributed to a variety of reasons, from frustration over all the historical and literary criticism encouraged in biblical reading, to a countercultural desire to slow down. By reading or hearing scripture without an agenda other than to be open to the Spirit, we free ourselves up for the movement of the Spirit and the surprises she may have in store for us.

The four stages of *Lectio Divina* are fairly simple. You read, meditate, express yourself to God, and rest in the Spirit. The passage you read should probably be a short one, no more than a few verses long. You might use part of a psalm or even just a line of Jesus' teachings. Once you have your passage, take a few centering breaths, and then begin.

LECTIO (READ). Read the passage slowly. Do not rush to get to the end. Take the time to read each and every word, letting each word sink down deep into your bones. Do not try to discern a meaning; don't worry about historical or literary context. Just read. Once you've read the passage through, pause for a moment, and then read it again. This time, read the words and note which word or phrase speaks to you. Is there a word that bothers you, a phrase that resonates with you?

MEDITATIO (MEDITATE). Let your mind ruminate over your word or phrase. Do images come to mind? Stories? What about memories? Sit for a while and let the Spirit move through the word or phrase. What might she be trying to say to you? What might this word mean for you in this moment, in this place? What might God be asking of you?

ORATIO (SPEAK). As you come to a sense of understanding, as the meaning this passage holds for you in this moment becomes clear (or even just a bit more in focus), lift your thoughts up to God. What do you want to express? Do you have any positive or negative reactions to what you've heard through your reading and meditating? Whether you wish to praise or pick a fight, be honest with God.

CONTEMPLATIO (CONTEMPLATE). Once you've offered your thoughts and feelings to the divine, rest. Simply be in God's presence for a while. Perhaps the divine voice will speak to you; perhaps you'll just enjoy the silence.

If you'd like to try this practice with a group of friends (it's a great practice for a small group), start by having one person read the passage out loud. Once you've read it through, have another person read the same passage. Listen as a group for the words or phrases that touch you individually. Reflect for a moment or two, and then share what you've each heard. As you share and listen, do not try to correct what anyone hears. Remember, the Holy One can speak through the same words in a variety of ways. Read the passage out loud again, and give yourself another few moments of reflection. Now share with each other your reactions to what you've personally heard from God. Once you've shared, spend time in individual contemplation. The person who first read may close with a small prayer after a few minutes of rest.

MEANT FOR THE STAGE

Not all of us are actors. We don't all particularly enjoy the limelight. So for those of us who dread the thought of lines and costumes and marks, this next practice may be a stretch—but hopefully, it'll be a good one. At the very least, it'll help you appreciate how the early Hebrew people and the first followers of Christ knew the sacred stories we share. The literacy rate in the ancient world was never high, and many of our written stories were first communicated orally. Even the works that were written down would have been read aloud. This suggests to us that if we only ever read scripture silently, never hearing it or even acting it out, then we're missing something.

To start out, simply grab a friend and take turns reading out loud to each other. That may sound a little strange, and it is at first. But once you get past the "this is sorta weird" self-conscious stuff, you're open to a rich experience. You can read any sacred text out loud, but the stories are probably the best place to start. Read from one of the Gospels or from the histories of Israel. Have one person read out loud while the other throws in appropriate sound effects. Just know, as you read through scripture this way, you might come across stories you've never noticed before (even if you think you've read the whole Bible).

Remember that story about Amy getting stuck in the book of Exodus? Turns out she never quite read through the whole thing until much, much later. It was spring semester, our third year of seminary. Graduation was mere weeks away. The assignment was to read the entire book of Acts in one sitting, so your intrepid authors took a seat on Teri's couch and proceeded to read aloud just as we've described, taking turns reading and providing sound effects. When we reached chapter 10, Teri began to read of Peter's vision of a sheet covered in animals. She soon noticed, however, that no appropriate sound effects were forthcoming, but she continued to read. About halfway through the story, Amy grabbed the Bible from Teri's hands and loudly proclaimed, "You are making that up! That is *not* in the Bible." Then she looked down to find that it was, in fact, in the Bible, at which point she sheepishly handed the book back and continued her sound-effects job.

Even though she could have sworn she'd read the whole dang thing by that point in her life, Amy discovered that some things hadn't registered during her reading (she was probably speed-reading, after all). It took hearing the Bible out loud to both learn and appreciate that story (which has since become a favorite).

If you don't have a friend that you think would be up for this practice, you can look into audiobook Bibles. Try *The Bible Experience* published by Zondervan; among other stellar actors, Samuel L. Jackson joins the project as the voice of God. Yeah, you read that right. Samuel L. mother-bleeping Jackson as God. That's just worth a listen, spiritual practice or not!

If you've tried reading out loud, experiment next with acting. Grab some props, costumes, and whatever else you think will enhance your fun and focus. We've acted out sacred stories several times, and were highly entertained each and every time. When you're going for the whole enchilada, it helps to pick a passage that will make you laugh (so the passion of Christ is probably out; the bloody fight scenes from Judges, 1 & 2 Samuel and 1 & 2 Kings are particularly good). Because, let's face it, you're being a teeny bit silly. And that's awesome. One friend of ours, dressed up with sword and crown, noted the similarities to this practice and some of the more ridiculous things he'd done as a church kid, stating, "Holy Youth Group Flashback, Batman!"[2] We were acting out the story of Jezebel and Ahab wherein the royal couple steal some land by murdering the rightful owner, and get a serious comeuppance (dogs licking up blood is involved—rather gross, but really amusing when the dog in your dramatized version is a fluffy toy poodle).[3] Some people might say that by engaging scripture in such a way, you remove its gravitas. We're fine with that. People have made Scripture feel so far removed from us, and from the entertaining and the silly, it's as though it can only be read or spoken in a very serious voice. If acting out stories and laughing while you do makes the sacred stories just a little more relatable and real, then we say it's a worthwhile spiritual practice.

EVERYTHING IS ILLUMINATED, AND EVERYONE CAN TELL A STORY

Back in the day (that'd be a pre-Gutenberg press day), biblical manuscripts wouldn't be as plain and text-centric as they are now. You'd have decorated borders, illustrations, and symbols everywhere. Letters at the beginning of paragraphs and sentences would be enlarged and embellished. The *Book of Kells* is one of the most well-known and well-preserved examples of an illuminated manuscript, and its art seems to influence tattoo designs all over. Monks who spent much of their lives copying holy words added these illustrations and flourishes, not just out of boredom or demand, but as a way to artistically reflect on the sacred stories being written. When we got the printing press, we gained access to the written word but we lost this spiritual practice.

To begin exploring the connection between art and sacred words, pick a passage and read through it a few times. In a similar vein to the *Lectio Divina* process, note which verse, phrase, or even just one word stands out to you the most. Take that verse and write it out on a piece of paper. Now, start doodling. Yes, doodling. Add flourish to the letters, if you like. Let your pen or pencil dance across the paper; feel what the scripture may be inspiring you to draw. You don't have to be an artist, or even an art-lover, to find this practice enriching. Neither of your authors can draw her way out of a paper bag, and yet we both enjoy a good doodle. Try writing your verse again, this time with artistic intent. What happens when you let each word find its own space and structure? What calls out to you from each

---

2. Joshua Dubinsky-Nabor. Staunton, Virginia. 9/8/08.
3. 1 Kings 21-22

word, each phrase? You may find as you draw that you discern deep meaning through your doodles. Or at the very least, you may find that you sense a connection to the artist God whose strange and wonderful creations include the okapi and the platypus.

Another creative way to engage scripture stems from ancient Jewish practice. While it may be seen as sacrilegious by some today, over the ages it has been a common practice to embellish on the sacred stories passed down to us. Fleshing out stories in our biblical canon, or even adding stories to fill in gaps, is known as *midrash* in the Jewish tradition. The writer of a *midrash* is trying to understand a sacred story better by imagining fuller background for a briefly-mentioned character, or a piece of action that seems to be missing in the story as written. A few lines of scripture can become a long dialogue; a nameless woman can get both a name and a story of her own. That's right, *midrash* is the most ancient form of fan fiction!

> Try writing some biblical fan fiction.

Try writing your own form of *midrash*, (or biblical fan fiction if you prefer). Find a story in the Bible you enjoy, one that's perhaps even very familiar to you. Now examine that story. Where might you expand? Is there a brief exchange between characters you could lengthen? What would they say? Or imagine yourself to be a character in that story (mentioned by name or just as a member of the faceless crowd). Reflect on the story from your character's perspective. What do you learn? What comes alive for you? Now think about what you've written. How might the Spirit be speaking to you through your own words as you have reflected on these sacred words?

> "I love to tell the story;
> 'tis pleasant to repeat
> what seems, each time I tell it,
> more wonderfully sweet."
> —FROM THE HYMN *I LOVE TO TELL THE STORY*,
> WORDS BY KATHERINE HANKEY

We are a story people. We bond over stories. We weep over them. We laugh over them. We live in and through them. We are shaped by them even as we shape them. The sacred stories we have been given are rich with meaning to be discovered and lived out. We have been given a really, really good narrative about God and the unfailing, uncompromising love the Divine One has for us. So go, live these stories out. Spend time with them.

Be encouraged and even challenged by them. Whatever you do, however you choose to engage scripture, do not let it remain only words on a page. Let the Spirit bring you to life even as she brings the scriptures to life for you and in you.

GOING TO PRACTICE
Pick a scripture passage. A favorite, one from the lectionary, something from a randomly-opened page, it doesn't matter. Write the passage out with colored markers. Use one color for people, one for places, one for verbs, one for inanimate objects, one for adjectives and adverbs. Does anything stand out to you? Is the passage verb-heavy, noun-heavy, object-heavy? If words are repeated, circle them. Now read the passage, one part of speech at a time. Does anything new stand out? Anything you hadn't noticed before?

SEE MORE...
The Bible. Really. Go read/listen to one.

TWO

IN THE FLESH

*"You put your whole self in, put your whole self out,
Put your whole self in and you shake it all about..."*

A quote floating around the web-o-sphere says we "aren't physical beings having a spiritual experience, we're spiritual beings having a physical experience."[1] The author is trying to get at the idea of *incarnation*—which literally means "in the flesh"—but while the sentiment is surely one of trying to help us live into our true selves, the language is still not quite right. The reality is that human beings, created in the image of God, can't be separated that way—we are mind/body/spirit, and without integration of these aspects of the whole, we ultimately find ourselves fragmented, missing out on the goodness God has in store for us. Interestingly, Pierre Teilhard de Chardin, who uttered this attempt at describing God's hope for us as incarnate beings made in God's image, managed to get closer with another statement: "There is neither spirit nor matter in the world; the stuff of the universe is *spirit-matter*."[2]

That's closer to the mysterious reality of being human. We are whole selves, not just a foot or a hand or a brain or a spirit, not just a job title or a relationship or a talent or a failing. So often we are asked to compartmentalize our lives in this way: we have separate boxes for friends, family, fun, and work—sometimes several boxes for each! Pop-religion has often encouraged this separation, asking us to keep sacred and secular apart, to make faith a matter for the mind, or worse, telling us check our brains

---

1. Pierre Teilhard de Chardin, *The Phenomenon of Man* (1938).
2. Pierre Teilhard de Chardin, *A Sketch of a Personalistic Universe* (1936).

at the door. Part of that separation has been a Platonist division between mind, spirit, and body, with the body always coming lowest on the totem pole. The physicality of our bodies is often looked down upon, blamed for being the home of those base desires that keep us from reaching our spiritual potential.

That Platonist division now underlies a culture that simultaneously idolizes and denigrates the body. On the one hand, we're constantly shown bodies that have been sculpted to perfection, either through computerized or dietary means, and we are encouraged to compare ourselves to that false perfection. On the other hand, we're taught to ignore our bodies—push through, walk it off, care more for our minds, be more than just a pretty face. Many of us have worked so hard at creating a body that's pleasing to others, we've forgotten how to simply live in this beautifully and wonderfully made body we have been gifted. Others of us have worked so hard at developing a mind that enables us to do amazing things that we've neglected our bodies, insisting they don't matter as much as what's on the inside. Add in the fact that 40% of people between the ages of 18 and 34 don't have health insurance,[3] so we have to ignore what our bodies are saying because we can't afford to do anything about it, and we have the trifecta of mind-body dualism.

Into this reality our spiritual traditions speak—of embodiment, of wholeness, of incarnation. The Abrahamic traditions refuse to be isolated in the mind. They insist on being lived with our whole selves: Judaism with *mitzvoth* that require bodily participation and engagement with the world, Christianity with the incredible theological claim that God literally became flesh and lived among us, and Islam with traditions that involve the whole body in prayer and in submission to God. In Hindu tradition, Vishnu also takes on physical form, and the various devotional practices often involve bodily movement. Few spiritual traditions divorce spirit and body the way Western culture has taught us to do.

Finding ways to be aware of, listen to, and fully inhabit our bodies is important for this world in which we are so internally divided. In a time marked by division and fragmentation, living fully integrated lives is one way to resist the forces that build barriers even while tearing us apart, and so lead our culture toward wholeness. There are lots of ways we can exercise our spirits as we live in flesh and bone.

Probably the most popular bodily-spiritual practice going right now is yoga. Whether it's traditional Hatha Yoga or the hot-room Bikram yoga,

---

3. Figure 4 in the "Overview of the Uninsured in the United States," from the Department of Health and Human Services, 2011, http://aspe.hhs.gov/health/reports/2011/CPSHealthIns2011/ib.shtml.

classes are overflowing and DVDs fly off the shelves. A major part of yoga practice is about breathing. The breathing of yoga practice is deliberate and deep, and flows into every part of your body. The breath itself is the core of the practice, and is in many ways the core of all spiritual practice. In the beginning God breathed the breath of life into us, according to many of our sacred texts. The air that flows in and out of our bodies is the very breath of God, bringing life to bodies that would otherwise be just flesh and bones.

> God is closer than breathing.

Take a moment to be aware of your breathing. Feel the air in your nostrils, in your lungs. Feel your chest rise and fall, feel your diaphragm (that muscle at the bottom of your rib cage whose spasms we call hiccups) contract and expand. Breathe deeply and slowly. Perhaps try some *ujjayi* breathing,[4] which creates a deep and soft sound as you inhale and exhale, bringing to mind the ocean and centering your thoughts. Just focus on the breath. If you do find your mind wandering, try reminding yourself that, as Alfred, Lord Tennyson, said, God is closer than breathing.[5] Every breath is sacred!

Many of us take up yoga simply as exercise, which is good and worthwhile. The strength and flexibility we can build through a yoga practice are important components of maintaining healthy bodies. We may find ourselves using yoga for exercise and discovering the spiritual aspects as we grow into practice. Participating in an exercise that has been practiced for millennia allows us to connect to something larger than ourselves and more ancient than our imaginations, to join a long line of people throughout the ages who have sought to be integrated mind-body-spirits. When we take a yoga class, we also join a community of people seeking that integration right here and now. In our experience, there's no judgment in a yoga class (as there often is in other exercise classes where you can watch other people). There are just people breathing together, moving together, stretching their bodies and their souls together. If you haven't tried it already, a yoga class may be just the thing to jump start your mind-body-spirit integration. It takes time and practice to learn to be aware of your body, what it's saying to you, how you can push it and when to take it easy, to learn to live fully *in* this God-given physical form, not just use it. Don't have time for a class, or not yet ready to take that plunge? There are some yoga videos that can get you off to a good start (see the resources at the end of the chapter for

---

4. "Conqueror Breath," *Yoga Journal,* http://www.yogajournal.com/poses/2485.
5. Alfred, Lord Tennyson, "The Higher Pantheism," in *From The Holy Grail and Other Poems* (London: Strahan, 1870).

our favorites), you can check out the Yoga Journal online for great beginner articles, and in a pinch you can even try out the yoga poses in Wii Fit to get a taste. Once you have a few poses down, you can try beginning your day with a simple practice that will get your blood flowing, your breath moving, and your spirit settled into your body for the day. You may find that a few minutes of yoga before you hop in the shower offers the centering in your image-of-God body that you need to go through the day without falling into the compartments our culture tries to impose.

One of the things Teri's yoga teacher says frequently is "get more grounded." Practicing yoga requires being aware of your body and its connection to the earth. It's a reminder that we came from dust, and to dust we shall return, but in between we have this gift of breathing God's breath and moving through God's space. Yoga can be a great way to gently push those muscles and joints until a new breath of life enters in. When we are more grounded in the body that inspired God to say "It was very good," we are also a part of deconstructing a culture of objectifying shame—both for human bodies and for the rest of God's good creation. When we feel the stretch, or find our balance, we turn off judgment. A famous yoga teacher reminds us that "Love is what's left when you let go of everything you don't need."[6] Imagine if we could incarnate love—if we could be love in the flesh—and how that might change the world around us.

Another exercise practice many have found quickly turning into a spiritual practice is running. (Walking is good too!) Getting moving, especially outside, can be a way to clear your mind, connect to nature, pound out your problems on the pavement, and work through both conscious and subconscious issues. Many of us already like to take our exercise outside, especially in the warmer months. Or our commute may include a bit of a walk (or a jog, for some of us who are chronically late). Try going for a walk or a run but leaving your iPod at home—just be aware of the sights and sounds around you, your own heart rate, the sound of your feet against the ground, the feel of the weather on your skin. Moving your body through physical space, whether at a walking pace or a sprint, can provide the backdrop for clarity of thought and connection to the Spirit all around—it just takes paying attention to what God is doing around you, and voila! your exercise time or the last few blocks from the parking garage to the office are a time for connecting to the divine energy that flows through even the most boring of spaces.

Not a runner? Try walking through your neighborhood and sending out good vibes to each house you pass, blanketing your town in prayer.

---

6. Erich Schiffmann, at the end of *Yoga Mind & Body* (Waner Home Video, 2003).

There aren't any right or wrong ways to do it, but sharing your spiritual energy with your neighbors, even if they don't know it, can be a wonderful way to engage your body and spirit with your physical surroundings and your larger community.

In a similar vein is one of our favorites—dancing! There's no special equipment required, and you don't even have to get all dressed up and pay a cover charge (unless you want to, of course!). Just put on some music at home, close the blinds if you need to, and let your body move right there in your kitchen, living room, or closet. You're following in the great tradition of folks like the prophet Miriam and that kid with the slingshot, David, who both danced before their maker in joy, in praise, and in David's case, in a loincloth.[7] Move that body—let the Spirit move—and just enjoy the sensations. Focus your attention on what you feel as you move. Neither of us could be considered smooth dancers, and yet we know how connected you can feel when your body is moving to the beat and it feels as though the music is flowing in and then right back out of you.

Speaking of connecting, give punching a go. Yup, punching, as in jab, cross, left hook, and it's a knockout! Except, of course, you're not knocking anyone out. Either with a heavy bag or a padded partner, wrap your hands and go through a few reps. As you throw your punches, try incorporating a piece of scripture or concentrating on a sacred image. This particular exercise is a great way to release stress, anger, and frustration, so images of fire or verses like "how long oh, Lord" (from Psalm 13) might be good. Focus on your holy image even as you concentrate on your punching; recite each word of your short scripture passage as you throw a punch. Amy's personal favorite combo includes Psalm 61:1 and goes like this: *Hear* *jab* *my* *jab* *cry* *right hook* *O* *left hook* *God* *backfist*.

Maybe all that cardio isn't your thing, or you need a lower-impact way to pray with your body. Try out different postures for prayer. The most stereotypical posture is to kneel and put your hands together—and maybe that works for you. That hands-clasped-in-prayer pose suggests that we hold on to our time with God, so we are not able to hold on to anything else. Lots of us are so used to bowing our heads (which was originally done in order to avoid visual distraction) or talking to God as we drift to sleep that something like kneeling can actually be a way to focus the mind. There are lots of other options, though. Thousands of years ago it was common to lift your face and palms to the sky while praying, as a symbol of willingness to be open to God's presence. Many people find that lying prostrate, forehead to the ground, helps them get into the right frame of mind to approach God.

---

7. Read about Miriam's grooving in Exodus 15:20 and David's busting a move in 2 Samuel 6.

Some traditions involve placing your hands on the thing you're praying for—praying for someone who had a heart attack? Put your hands on your heart. Praying for relief from mental illness? Put your hands on your head. Praying for someone who broke a hip? You get the idea.

Are you with a group of people? Try standing in a circle and putting your left hand on the shoulder of the person next to you—in this way the circle is connected and we're reminded that we are not alone, the hands of both God and our community help guide and sustain us. Or use what we often call "thumbs up and to the left"—everyone in the circle give the two-thumbs-up sign, then turn your hands to the left and open your palms, so you have one hand facing up and the other down. Clasp hands in this position, and you'll be both supporting and being supported.

> *"We always think spiritual experiences should be*
> *peaceful and relaxing—*
> *is it possible to have a spiritual experience where*
> *you're squirming and uncomfortable?"*
> —THE REV. ELSA PETERS[8]

It may feel uncomfortable to touch others while you're praying. If you are uncomfortable, listen to that feeling. If it is rooted in feeling unsafe, don't do it. If it's not about safety, but about wanting to remain distant from others, try to think of some ways to safely cross that bridge. Prayers like the ones described above, touching the shoulder or hand, can be good ways to begin. In our world we so rarely touch people in non-sexual or non-commodified ways, it can be hard to remember that we are created physical beings. We have heard stories of people who go to church primarily because the time of passing the peace (which usually involves handshakes) is the only time they are able to touch and be touched—the rest of their lives are so isolated. If your life is isolated in that way, look for some ways to experience the soft touch of the Holy through the physical touch of others—handshakes, friendly hugs, pats on the back.

THE TWO ENDS OF THE MODERATION SPECTRUM...

Normally when we think of faith practices, indulging ourselves is not near the top of the list. Instead we hear more about either practicing moderation or about fasting. These are good practices—and when combined with the occasional experience of extravagance, they can be even more profound.

---

8. Uttered in a conversation over cheese, bread, and wine at a vineyard in Sonoma, 4/9/12.

Getting a pedicure or massage are great opportunities to experience indulgence as a spiritual moment. Not only is it a time when someone physically and lovingly cares for you, it can also be a moment of experiencing the extravagant love of God. Yes, it often feels like an unattainably expensive luxury, but occasionally those can be good for our spirits too (as long as they don't get us into debt). The growth in the spa industry during the recession at the beginning of the 21st century strongly suggests that there's a craving here that goes beyond pampering.[9] Whenever you do indulge, sink into the relaxation a massage, pedicure, or other luxury brings. As stress is relieved and pressure points attended to, let go of the burdens that weigh on you. Offer them up to God, say goodbye, and soak up your moment of physical and spiritual release.

At the other end of the spectrum, fasting is a practice that reminds us that we are not ultimately in control of everything. Not many of us are fond of fasting. Going *without* is not a part of the 21st century Western psyche. But it can be an important way to connect with our bodies as well as with other members of God's worldwide family. We have become a people very proud of our self-sufficiency and independence, but fasting helps us keep our balance in life.[10] It also helps us see ourselves as we really are. When we remove something, we quickly see how much we depend on it, how much it controls us. Deciding to go without—whether we go without food, television, cell phone, iPod, video games, or anything else we use regularly—we learn how much our peace depends upon the pleasures we get as a result of these things, and how powerful and clever the body and mind are at getting their own way against our strong resolves.[11]

Fasting is intended to be a time of re-centering ourselves toward God— to allow the physical hunger to remind us that we were not actually created to be self-sufficient, but rather interdependent. It can also remind us of our connection and interdependence with others in the world. When we go without food, we remember those who are hungry. When we go without something we love and use every day, we remember those who make our material goods. When we fast from some of the distractions of modern life, we remember those for whom there is no distraction possible.

So try it out—maybe for just part of a day at first, working up to a whole day or even a whole week, depending on what your fast entails. Whether you choose to fast from food, from snacking between meals, from text messaging, from television, from expressing negative thoughts,

9. Bruce Grindy, "2011 Economic Snapshot: Salon/Spa Industry Vibrant, Growing Economic Sector," Probeauty Association, July 18, 2011, http://probeauty.org/news/progress/2011/07/18/2011-economic-snapshot-salonspa-industry-vibrant-growing-economic-sector/.

10. Richard Foster, *Celebration of Discipline* (San Francisco: HarperSanFrancisco, 1978), 56.

11. Dallas Willard, *Spirit of the Disciplines* (San Francisco: HarperSanFrancisco, 1991), 166.

or anything else, the key to the practice is to simply do it, and to do it without judgment. If you forget and grab your phone, pop a few Pringles, or let your snark out, just notice and commit to trying again. Use the moments you feel deprived or constrained to pay attention to what your spirit is saying. What is the deeper need you want to fill? Direct your attention to the Spirit rather than to your desire, and see where that leads you.

WHEN YOU'RE NOT FASTING...

...you have to eat! Eating can be just as much a spiritual practice as fasting, and it's something we do every day, so take the opportunity to bring the Holy with you. As with many practices, that starts with awareness and mindfulness. What we choose to put in our bodies, where it comes from, who produces it and how they are treated, how it gets to us, how its production affects the earth—these are all spiritual matters. Making these choices is one way we can remind ourselves that we're part of God's greater interconnected world, and how we behave in that system matters.

Take a moment to think about your favorite meal, or about the meal right in front of you. What are its component parts? Trace the origins of your food and take a moment to offer thanks for the earth, the farmers, the laborers who harvest or process, the transport workers, and anyone else involved in making that meal possible. How does feeding your body affect other bodies—of workers, children, animals, water systems, the delicate balance of the earth? It's eye-opening for many of us to think so deeply about our food, since most of us nowadays just get our food from the store or restaurant without putting in the work and worry that goes with growing food. As you eat, be aware of what you are putting into your body and how you are part of this beautiful and productive web of life, and as much as you are able, be sure that what you use to feed your body does not harm other bodies.

> "I partake of many traditions' spiritual practices,
> and I enjoy all of their bread."
> —ELINOR PISANO[12]

Nearly every spiritual tradition involves food at some level. Whether feasting or fasting or symbolic, eating together is at the core of community. When we gather around a table, we share something of ourselves as we

---

12. Uttered in a conversation over cheese, bread, and wine at a vineyard in Sonoma, 4/9/12.

enjoy the bounty of the earth. The food and the stories intertwine to create a complete, multi-sensory experience.

Next time you have a meal, let all your senses in on the journey. What do you see—color, texture, presentation? What do you hear—sizzling, bubbling, silence? What do you smell—sweet, savory, veggies, meat? Is the plate hot, or maybe chilled? All before you even taste, you've already been on a journey through the wonder of creativity and abundance, even if you're just having a cheese quesadilla or a bowl of soup. Now it's time to let the taste buds have their turn too—dig in! Notice how all your senses intermingle to allow your taste buds to do their job. Be sure you chew slowly and let your whole mouth join the party, as there are some tastes that you can only sense if they come in contact with certain parts of your mouth. Be sure to keep breathing as you chew, as smell and taste are senses that work together, and because often a little air can change the way things taste. Savor the moment, the feeling of being provided for (even if you cooked it yourself), the opportunity to let yourself be nourished. Eating is one of the great pleasures God has given us—enjoy that gift with your whole self.

If you're having a meal with people, talk about your experience and the feelings it brings up. Does the dessert smell like Grandma's kitchen? Does the color of the entrée take you right back to a birthday dinner your Dad grilled just for you? Does this sauce remind you of the first time you tried to cook in college, only to call home desperate for advice? Share those stories as you eat, and let them enhance everyone's meal. Whether you're in a fancy restaurant trying out the chef's tasting menu or sitting on the floor of a new furniture-less apartment eating pizza, joining your stories with your sensory experience can transform a meal from just something to feed your stomach into a spirit-filled encounter with the Holy.

In many religious traditions, breaking bread together is a symbol of community, of forgiveness and hope, and of love shared across boundaries. In the Christian tradition, when we break bread together we proclaim that we break down the borders we see—ethnicity, age, gender, socio-economic status, living and dead, time and space. When the bread is broken and shared, we who partake are then re-membered—we put back together the community of God's people. It is a beautiful idea: sharing a meal can literally put together the community, can bring wholeness where before there was division. Of course, that beautiful idea only becomes reality if we actually do share meals across boundaries, not just with people who look and think like us. Sometimes that begins by simply trying a food from a different culture. Sometimes it might begin by volunteering at a shelter or community kitchen, and actually sitting down and eating with the guests who need those programs. Sometimes it might begin by traveling to another part of the country or world and seeing who you can meet. Whatever the first step is, we urge you to take it! You might just find that God is already waiting there, hoping that your eyes will be opened and you'll see a spirit-moment as you break the naan, croissant, pita, challah, tortilla, pretzel roll, rice cake, roti, gluten-free baguette, or even Wonder Bread.

...AND BEFORE YOU SUCCUMB TO THE FOOD COMA...

Many of us have an internal monologue about our bodies that would put mudslinging politicians to shame. With all the messages about perfection coming at us all the time, and the dearth of normal body images in the media, we may occasionally look at ourselves and wonder why we got stuck with this body anyway. Sometimes it doesn't work quite right, sometimes it's pudgy in the wrong places and skinny in other wrong places, sometimes our skin breaks out or we have the worst hair day ever. In those moments, and in every moment really, what we say to ourselves matters. If your internal monologue features any put-downs, comparisons, or frustration about your body, now is a good time to try to think of ways to change that. You might start with one of the breathing exercises we talk about in chapter 8 and use as your focus phrase "I am wonderfully made" or "created in the image of God."

The only time negative self-talk is part of any of our spiritual traditions is when we have misunderstood them. Throughout the sacred texts, the goodness of creation and created beings is affirmed. Sure, we don't always (or even usually) live into that goodness, but some of that is because we have become disconnected from our Source. Take a moment to listen to the things God has to say about creation—which includes your body! The overwhelming reality is love: "And behold, it was very good" (Gen. 1:31). Maybe even take a look at yourself in the mirror, clothing optional. What do you see? Can you see the divine image? It may feel cheesy to talk to yourself in the mirror, but it's one of the few opportunities you have to get a positive message about your body. Let your voice be the voice of God, affirming that you are beautiful, loved, and reflective of God's glory, no matter how you stack up to the latest magazine cover or TV star. The more you remind yourself that people see something holy when they look at you, the more holiness you're likely to shine, and the more connected you'll be to that holy perfection that underlies all of creation.

In these ways we are able to connect our wordy intellectual prayers with the bodies we have been gifted by the Divine, and we open ourselves to new holy experiences when we refuse to keep our spirits locked away in our brains. We put together a whole integrated life, and soon find ourselves living our prayers in every movement we make. When the Bible says, "now you are the body of Christ" (1 Cor. 12:27), that means that our bodies are somehow involved in showing Christ to the world. Teresa of Avila put it beautifully back in the 16th century when she wrote, "Christ has no body now on earth but yours—no hands but yours, no feet but yours,"[13] so let's get our hands, our feet, our whole selves involved in the search for the Spirit!

GOING TO PRACTICE

Put together a snack including your favorite savory and sweet items. Enjoy your sweet treat while reading from Psalm 119: "How sweet are your words to my taste, sweeter than honey to my mouth!" (v. 103). Eat your savory dish as you read from Psalm 34: "O taste and see that the LORD is good; happy are those who take refuge in him" (v. 8).

Take a moment to bring to mind something that reminds you of God's abundant grace. Let that image or word settle over the images of scarcity, fear, and judgment that are so often at the core of how we think about our bodies or our world—cover them with grace.

Sometimes we get so caught up in the competition of the world,
in the idea of scarcity, in the constant coming and going...
    Sometimes we get so caught up in the images of judgment
        in the certainty that we have to create our own good
            in the feeling of distance...
We forget that God is Love
    that God is Good
        that there is enough for everyone
        that all our senses can show us God's hope for the world.

Let your taste buds help the sacred text to come alive!

SEE MORE...

Doug Pagitt and Kathryn Prill, *BodyPrayer: The Posture of Intimacy with God* (Colorado: Waterbrook Press, 2005).

Thomas Ryan, *Reclaiming the Body in Christian Spirituality* (Paulist Press, 2005).

Nancy Roth, *Spiritual Exercises: Joining Body and Spirit in Prayer* (Seabury Books, 2005).

---

13. "St. Teresa of Avila," http://www.rc.net/southwark/ashfordstteresa/St%20Teresa%20of%20Avila.htm

THREE

WONDER AS I WANDER

*"Lord, I don't know where all this is going,
or how it all works out..."*

—NEWSBOYS[1]

"**D**on't Just Do Something, Stand There," a headline boldly states in
the August 2011 *Los Angeles Times*.[2] The article underneath the
headline discussed the scientific value of purposelessness in terms
of increased creativity and productivity. The accepted premise
highlighted something we already know—that we are beyond
busy. Many of us wear our busyness as a badge of honor, proclaiming our
packed schedules and lack of free time as if it correlates with our amazing-
ness or our productivity. We accept the mantra that time spent without a
tangible result is time wasted.

Unfortunately, the article points out, wasted time is also creative time.
Our best thoughts often come when we're not thinking specifically about
the topic at hand. Creative energy flows best when we slow our bodies and
our minds down. Staring out the window, eyes out of focus, daydream-
ing—when we catch ourselves doing these things we feel guilty for wasting
time, but that *feel guilt, stop dreaming, go back to something 'productive'* cycle
also blocks the spirit of creativity. These apparently time-wasting activities
can be conduits connecting us to the creative energy that flows throughout
the universe.

---

1. Newsboys. *Lord (I Don't Know)*. Sparrow. 2002. CD.
2. Christian McEwan, "Don't Just Do Something, Stand There," *Los Angeles Times*, August 14, 2011.,
http://www.latimes.com/news/opinion/commentary/la-oe-mcewen-donothing-20110814.

Carrie Newcomer's song "I Meant To Do My Work Today" is a great example of how we can reframe this "wasted" time as prayer. She sings about her great intentions to get the whole to-do list done, save the world, and still have time to clean the house, but she "got waylaid by the morning sun" and "silence called me deeper still." The sounds and sights of nature—birds calling, the moon shining cool and bright—capture her attention and she loses herself in the moment, wandering through her thoughts and catching glimpses of the holy she might otherwise have missed.

Ever had that kind of experience?

Whether you spend your days rushing around trying to stay focused every moment, or sitting at the table wondering how the whole day seems to have passed without a single to-do-list item getting crossed off, this practice of losing yourself in the moment can be a wonderful way to connect with the Spirit. Next time you catch yourself longing to stare out the window instead of at your computer screen, go for it. Soften your gaze, let your eyes just rest on whatever might be out there, and see what comes up in your mind and imagination. Notice the way the wind moves the leaves on the tree, the way the sunlight reflects off the snow, the antics of squirrels. When the flames in the fireplace are more enticing than the words on the page or the screen, just let yourself get sucked in to their dance. Allow yourself to be waylaid by the morning sun or kept awake by the cool bright moon.

One of the primary ways many of us know God is as Creator. "In the beginning, God created" are the very first words of the Bible, after all! That creative energy still moves, still creates and re-creates, so the least we can do is notice once in a while. Staring out the window, watching a sunset, wondering what those birds are up to on that power line—these are all potential ways to sense the spirit of God moving in the world. Sometimes letting your mind wander can be a way to hear the still small voice of God, whispering in your ear. Sometimes it can be a way to make space for something new to happen. Sometimes it's just the break your brain needs to see a new way forward on a problem or a project. However you experience those moments, rest in them and be grateful for the gift. It's not wrong to take a brain-break; only to feel guilty about it. Much like the practice of Sabbath, just letting your mind wander and your eyes sweep over whatever is around you or outside your window is a gift, a rest for an overworked mind in an overworked culture, an acknowledgement that we do not do life on our own and the world will go on while we sit in the beauty of the earth for a few moments.

Not long after that *Los Angeles Times* article, another article made the rounds of the Internet. Titled "What Happened to Downtime?"[3] it asked

---

3. Scott Belsky, "What Happened to Downtime?" http://the99percent.com/articles/6947/What-Happened-to-Downtime-The-Extinction-of-Deep-Thinking-Sacred-Space.

us to make a practice out of protecting our sacred space of not-doing. As we look forward to a day when we can even be productive in the shower, our last remaining space for deep thought is on the brink of extinction. How many of us have had ideas come to us in the shower, or just when we're waking up or falling asleep, or while we're driving through a dead-cell zone? Protecting that space—space where we aren't expected to get things done or to be perfect—becomes a holy task. How can we encounter God's still small voice if our lives are constantly packed with activity and productivity and expectation?

One small rebellion against that expectation to be always "on" is to take a few minutes to let your mind wander. Wonder about what you see or what thoughts appear in your head. Follow that chipmunk with your eyes. Spend a few minutes every day doing nothing—just letting your imagination go where it will. And don't get a phone in your shower—you need that space! It's one of the most holy, creative spaces left in our wired world. The loss of those spaces, the loss of the ability to let our minds wander off, the loss of downtime—these may very well equal the loss of creativity in our culture. The greatest inventions have often been germs of ideas that sprouted in wasted time. The greatest novels and movies and music and the solutions to nagging scientific questions came from wandering minds and long showers. So take a few minutes to let go, and see where the Spirit leads you when you let her take the reins.

If we can't take time to let our minds wander, it's unlikely we will take the time to think deeply, either—we're so connected through phones and computers and social media that our brains are losing the ability to focus on one thing for any length of time. How many of us have said some variation of "I can't pay attention that long" or "I lost my focus"? Though we may look like experts at multi-tasking, our brains don't actually do more than one thing at a time—we just switch rapidly back and forth. Teri noticed this recently when on retreat in a place with no Internet service. The little twitter icon in the menu bar never turned blue once during the whole week—what with no internet and all—but that didn't stop her eyes from flicking up there every minute or so to see if there were new messages. It quickly became clear just how distracting that can be—because if it had turned blue, you can bet she would have clicked over to see what was going on, and lost her train of thought on whatever work she was doing, whatever she was reading, or whatever she was trying to think about.

Learning to shut out the distractions and think deeply about things, to follow trains of thought to their logical conclusions, to follow rabbit trails and see what new places they might take us—these are not only essential skills for work or school, but for life with the divine, too. Just as our relationships with other people are shallow if we don't pay attention, our relationship with God can never go deeper if we only skim the surface before being distracted by the next thing. Let your mind wander and then follow those paths wherever they might lead, and you may find not just deeper thinking but also a deeper relationship with God.

If you're looking for something that seems more like what we often think of as traditional prayer, but not so structured that you have to remember what to say next, try a stream-of-consciousness prayer. Start with a few deep breaths, and give thanks for the breath that animates all of life. From there, let your mind go where it will. Whatever comes up, offer it to God. It may be a concern, a problem, a joy, it may be a person or a place, a news article you read, a photo you saw, a call you missed. There are no wrong prayers here—no wrong words, no wrong images. Give it to God as it comes up, and let your mind go wherever it wants to go next. We all know our subconscious (and our conscious, for some of us!) can be very bizarre, making connections and associations and leaps that we barely understand. Let your mind roam, and take God with you. You may find that you hear back from God, or you may not. Again, don't judge yourself or the things that come up—just be in the moment with the Spirit.

> Let your mind roam, and take God with you.

At the heart of all these practices is the idea of being in the moment with God, rather than dwelling in the past or anticipating the future. As Oogway says in *Kung Fu Panda*: "the past is history, tomorrow is a mystery, but today is a gift—that is why it is called the present." Cutesy, yes, but true! The present moment is a gift we have been given, and our act of gratitude is to live in it. We cannot change the past, we cannot control what might happen tomorrow, but we can rest in this moment, however imperfect it might be. We can be aware of God's presence in the now, allowing the living Word to speak into our current situation, noticing the breath of the Spirit moving. Best of all, it's easy to try—and to try again and again until it becomes a habit!

Looking for God in the moment is as simple as, well, looking for God in *this* moment. Whether you're reading, jogging, working, or out for a drink with friends, be aware. Let this moment be enough. Picture yourself surrounded by the light of God's presence, and rest there. It's an invisible prayer that can suffuse any moment, no matter what you are doing. When we're busy rushing around planning the next thing, it's easy to miss the little things. When Paul writes urging us to "pray without ceasing" (1 Thess. 5:17), he could mean something as simple as being aware of God in every moment. To live with a consciousness of the presence of God makes everything a prayer, however imperfect, however difficult or easy, however frustrating or joyful.

WE INTERRUPT YOUR REGULARLY SCHEDULED PLAN

Lots of people describe themselves as "very go-with-the-flow." Some people truly are that way, but many of us just like to think of ourselves that way when the reality is a bit different. Instead, we might better be described as "go-with-the-flow-when-the-flow-looks-pretty-darn-close-to-my-plan." We like our illusion of control, the idea that somehow we're able to lay a plan and follow it—or, even better, the idea that we can make a plan and others (or even the world!) will follow it. Just thinking about these things brings to mind a statement we've heard more times than we can count: "if you want to make God laugh, tell God your plans." The fact that this statement has been so often uttered in our presence will tell you that we're part of the majority who likes things to go according to plan.

> "Life is what happens to you while you're busy making other plans."
> —JOHN LENNON

There can be something beautiful about recognizing that we are not the author of the plan. Sure, it's hard (ridiculously so for some of us) but it is possible to *become* a person who goes with the flow, to train ourselves to see where the Spirit is moving and go there, rather than always insisting on following the map we've laid out, whether that map is for a day, an event, or a lifetime. That doesn't mean never getting anything done, it doesn't mean laying aside ambition or goals or dreams, it doesn't mean accepting the status quo and never working for justice or peace because that doesn't seem part of the flow. But it does mean sometimes letting go of the best laid plans we're constantly trying to follow and following the Spirit instead. Occasionally she will lead us to places or activities or work or ideas we would never have considered. Usually she will lead us exactly where we need to go. She might lead us to exactly the opposite of where we wanted to go. None of these are inherently bad (unless you follow what you think is the Spirit and end up hurting others, yourself, or the planet). The point of the practice is to learn how to let go just a little bit so that God can move in your life and in the life of the world—not to wander aimlessly through life never doing anything.

We'll be the first to confess that we're not good at this practice. We don't have lists of goals for each year of life, but we do have some pretty specific ideas about what the world should look like. Though our ideas are founded in what we've learned from Scripture and through prayer, we still have to admit that they're ours and we don't want to let go of them. Nor should we let go of ideals like living in a world of peace and justice, a world where no one goes hungry, a community that cares for people and the environment, relationships that are loving and respectful. But how we get there is open for debate. The ways we might want to work for justice, the process for building a community, the method through which we ensure that no one is hungry, the plan for saving the planet—these are places where it would do us all good to let go of our control, even for just a few minutes.

For a day, or half a day, or an hour, can you contemplate the possibility of going with God's flow rather than your perfectly formed plans? This practice begins not with action, but with awareness—noticing the places or situations or times when we are frustrated that things don't seem to be going according to plan. Often those are moments when we are pushing against the flow. At first it's enough just to notice. After you've learned to notice those places, it's likely you'll want to look for a pattern to when the plan and the flow butt heads. You can look for that if you want, or you can try practicing a little internal letting go. The next time it happens, make a decision inside yourself to look for the movement of the Spirit in that frustrating moment. Then, when you've become practiced at looking for that movement, you can decide to follow it the next time. And voila, you'll soon find yourself going with the flow occasionally! Granted, it may not be the flow our friends or colleagues have in mind, it may not be the flow of traffic on the path of life, but it will be the flow that matters.

ALL WHO WANDER...

Some people have special talents: making balloon animals, nose-whistling, tweeting while walking. Amy has a particular talent for getting lost. Really, really lost. So lost that she once found herself miles away from the grocery store that was only one mile away from her house—the same grocery store where she worked and thus drove to several times a week. Given her talent, Amy has had plenty of opportunities to discover that getting lost can actually be a good experience. She's not the only one; heck, there's a TV show about finding yourself while *Lost*. Getting lost can be an adventure; you can find really good restaurants, bars, used bookstores, parks. When you seek to get lost, give yourself some time. Be safe and smart. If there are areas that may not be safe, know where they are so you can be intentional on whether or not your lost journey includes those areas. Rushing to work is not a good time for your spiritual exploration. You want to be feeling as comfortable as possible while becoming uncomfortable as you lose your way.

Now go. Turn off your GPS. Don't pay too much attention to the subway maps. Allow yourself to experience your own town anew. Discover a new favorite spot. On streets you're familiar with, look with open eyes to take in all those little nooks and crannies and alleyways you've never noticed before. In the places you've never or rarely been, let yourself be filled with curiosity. As you explore, remember that all roads really do lead somewhere. Whether or not you find how all your town's roads connect, or discover that beautiful old mansion at the end of a long and winding road, you've discovered that there is more, always more, to know, to see, to experience. Even if you didn't have a well-planned purpose in traveling, you may come to some wonderful destinations. The practice of getting lost may work within you in a way you'd never imagine. As you purposefully wander, perhaps you'll be strengthened for encounters with those non-planned moments in your life.

Travel as spiritual practice is an ancient idea. Across centuries and across faith traditions, people have left behind their homes and families and struck out on pilgrimages. Unlike the practice of getting lost, a pilgrimage often has a final destination in mind—usually a holy site. While the time at the holy site itself is certainly powerful, the journey there is often just as meaningful—if not more so. On the journey, friends are made, hardships endured, and the Holy encountered. The intentionality of a pilgrimage combined with the power of dislocation provides meaningful openness before God.

If you're intrigued by the possibility of going on a pilgrimage and are a part of a faith community, see if your organization (either at the local, regional, or national level) has an opportunity. Quite a few do. If you don't have that opportunity or would like to do something a little more independent, create your own pilgrimage. Pick sites that hold some sort of intrigue or meaning for you. Put together an itinerary that leaves room for unplanned moments. Invite friends to join and let your whole trip—the sights, the travel, the camaraderie—be a chance to meet God.

A traditional pilgrimage isn't for everyone. It's not always attractive and it's often not viable for those of us who don't have tons of vacation time. Centuries ago, the church realized this too. The ancient symbol of a labyrinth began to be incorporated into medieval cathedrals. No, we're not talking about that weirdly awesome David Bowie movie, nor about a maze with dead ends and wrong turns. A labyrinth is a circular path with only one way in that is also the way out, with paths that never cross. While no clear records exist about the use of such symbols, it is thought that by walking the labyrinth a person could imitate a pilgrimage to Jerusalem.[4] Though many church labyrinths were destroyed over the years, some survived (including the stunning one at Chartres Cathedral in France) to give later generations inspiration for a revival. For a society that loathes and at the same time revels in its busyness, the labyrinth offers a place to unwind. For people who feel as though they are adrift in life, no direction, no purpose, the labyrinth serves as an embodiment of the hope that the wandering may actually be leading somewhere after all. Walking the circular path, somehow never crossing your previous path, and always reaching the center, *you* become centered. Centered in God, in prayer.

Thanks to increased interest in labyrinths over the past few decades, you can find them in many locations. Whether outside or indoors, permanent or temporary, a labyrinth creates sacred space. As you walk the path, you seek out the way. Come to the labyrinth not to escape the world but to find your center and come back to the world. When you stand at the entrance of the labyrinth, offer a small prayer. Check your rushing self at the beginning. As you walk the path, enter into conversation with God. Offer up what you're seeking as you walk to the center. You might pause at every turn, take a deep breath, be intentionally slow. When you get to the center, take time to listen. Sit for a while if you like. Know peace as you listen for the still small voice of God. When you leave the center, walking in reverse the same path you took in, take with you the peace of the One who is our center.

It can be hard to let go of our conviction that we know just how things ought to go. It's hard to set the plan down for a moment, because we've heard too many horror stories of what happens to people who get off the track. If we aren't working the plan at every moment, we might never get a job or a promotion; we might miss the opportunity of a lifetime because we weren't quite qualified. But if we don't step off the hamster wheel for a moment, if we don't take the opportunity to get lost or go on pilgrimage or stare out the window and just see where the wind blows, we may find we've missed life, not just an opportunity. Noticing where your thoughts wander, what your eyes rest on, or what your subconscious has to say are important ways of connecting to what the Spirit is doing in your life—it's rare to get a communiqué all nicely typed in perfect memo format, but the gentle whisper comes and goes, bringing creativity, fresh hope, and deep connection, if only we will take a moment to listen.

---

4. Donna Schaper and Carole Ann Camp, *Labyrinths from the Outside In* (Woodstock, VT: Skylight Paths Publishing, 2000), 6.

GOING TO PRACTICE

Spend 3 minutes listening to Carrie Newcomer's song mentioned in this chapter (*I Meant To Do My Work Today*, on the
album *Before and After*). Then spend the same amount of
time—just 3 minutes—wandering through your own thoughts
and seeing where they take you. Next time, try a few more
minutes, until you're up to 10 minutes at a time just resting in
the presence of God and seeing where the Spirit leads you.

SEE MORE...

Check out the world labyrinth locator at www.labyrinthloca-
tor.com. If you can't find a labyrinth near you, you can try
using a handheld labyrinth or a finger labyrinth. Just Google
either term and go from there!

FOUR

≈

THE SOUND OF THE SACRED

"...Music is intrinsically spiritual, the sacred is intrinsically musical, and both music and the divine permeate every imaginable part of life."
—TERESA L. REED[1]

I t's been a long day and you're not home quite yet. You turn on the radio as you're driving down the highway. The song ends and the DJ puts on a new track, one you haven't heard before. The first beats play, a voice enters the song, a chorus sings out and suddenly, it's like this song is being played just for you. Somehow the DJ knew you'd be listening and knew what you needed to hear and now your day's stress is melting away. You find yourself nodding along (since you don't know the words yet) and making an attempt at harmonizing. You have to join in somehow, for you find that in this song, in the words, in the tune, your spirit has become part of something even greater.

Music is powerful. Whether it's a new song or an old favorite you put on repeat, music can change you. A song plays and the notes dance through the waves of sound into your being. They reach you, reach into you, and draw out deep emotions. They can delight, intrigue, heal, even hurt. Some say mathematics is the language of the universe, and while we won't argue with that, we will suggest that our universe may be bilingual. We've heard it said that our universe has a song that we sing, echoed in our

---

1. While Reed is speaking specifically about music in the West African context, we like to hope such a sentiment can be applied to our lives as well. Teresa L. Reed, *The Holy Profane: Religion in Black Popular Music* (Lexington: University of Kentucky Press, 2003), 5.

lives. Others say we each have our own individual song, and we learn to play in harmony with one another.

However you imagine music to be infused in our very beings, there can be little doubt that it is. You don't have to be gifted musically to find that playing an instrument has power or meaning for you. Music transcends language, experiences, culture. No, not everyone is going to love your favorite indie punk band but nearly everyone connects to music on some level. It's one of those things that make us human.

Music is also one of those things that help us connect with the divine. Some of the world's oldest music was written to express devotion, praise, concern, and thanksgiving to the heavens. When people couldn't find the simple words to express their need or praise or devotion to their deities, they turned to music. In the Judeo-Christian tradition, Miriam's Song is considered to be some of the oldest, if not *the* oldest, poetry in the Hebrew Bible.[2] She sings, she dances, she breaks out the tambourine to celebrate her people's deliverance from slavery in Egypt via that famous parting of the Red Sea.

Through the notes, the rhythms, the cadence, the tone, relationships are built—between you and the instrument, between you and the artist, between you and those listening or playing with you, between you and God. Music can help you focus and bring you into that sacred space where the veil between the Creator and the created is thin. It allows you to connect to the creative force that pervades the universe. It can inspire you to create and to express and to just be with delight! It can help you heal and to find catharsis and to gain peace. All done in the presence of the One who gave us the notes to sing, to play, to hear.

Engaging music can allow you to be emotional without having to pinpoint that emotion. Sometimes through the words or the sound a memory is triggered, relating to the first time you heard a particular song or to a time in your life where that song was your soundtrack. Whenever we, your authors, work with a family to plan a memorial service or funeral, one of the things we advise on is the music. Whatever songs are chosen for the service where you say goodbye and celebrate the life of your loved one, you will never forget hearing them in that context. Whenever you hear those songs again, you will very likely be taken back to that service and the myriad feelings running through you. Same goes for weddings or other emotionally charged events. We have a rolodex of emotions associated with different pieces of music. How many other things in our lives can we say that about? And how much of the emotion reflected in our music choices can we, or do we, share with God?

---

2. Exodus 15:21

Simply paying attention to your emotions and your music is a great way to begin your musical journey with the divine. Think about some of your favorite songs. Some may have absolutely nothing to do with your journey with God (if your guilty pleasure is still the *Macarena*, you might not find anything particularly meaningful there). But take time to reflect on the songs that do touch you and speak to you, the ones that capture you when they come on the radio or you find yourself playing over and over again. Look at the lyrics. Is there something in there that sounds like a plea, a thanksgiving, a prayer? You might be surprised to discover that some of your favorite songs have been unintentional prayers. May we suggest you make them intentional? Take note of certain songs that speak to different moods or needs you have. Listen for a song that expresses your need for friendship or your desire for direction or your rejoicing in milestones. Read through the lyrics as a prayer or just listen to the song. When you want to express something to the Holy One, to have a conversation even, invite God to come and enjoy some music with you. Also keep your ears open to the ways in which God may be trying to reach out to you through music. That song that jumps out of the stereo and grabs your spirit—maybe there's Someone trying to get your attention. Maybe it's a coincidence, maybe not. Be open to the words and melodies you hear as potential vehicles for grace.

While you're thinking about the music you like, spend time coming up with some playlists. Got a workout playlist? Great. Ready to push play on the tunage you want for studying? Fantastic. Add to those playlists for different needs, moods, feelings. Need to feel peace? Put together a list of songs that calm you down. It's been said that music with 60 beats per minute (ambient, slower classical, etc.) helps calm you down—physiologically, your body adjusts to the music, bringing you the peace you're seeking. Life's small (or large) injustices infuriating you? Make sure you have a righteous anger playlist. A little Bob Dylan, Rage Against the Machine, Adele, Nine Inch Nails, Ani DiFranco, Slayer—whatever works for you. Feel the need for community? Put together songs that make you think of your family or friends or college or whomever and wherever you feel surrounded by love and care. Open yourself to the power of the Spirit who is the bringer of peace, the seeker of justice, the creator of community.

Speaking of playlists—one of the exercises both of us enjoy doing with church groups is to explore our spiritual journeys by creating a playlist. What song expresses your faith life as a child? Did you grow up in a household where you went to church every Sunday? Perhaps your childhood song would be something like *This Little Light of Mine*. Did you grow up enjoying lazy weekends, or sporty ones, with no official religious exposure? Perhaps your childhood song would be that tune your mom hummed while she kicked back or your favorite version of "Take Me Out to the

Ballgame." What about growing up? Ever have a period of serious doubts? How about a moment where you felt God's presence more profoundly than you had ever imagined? Reflect on the various stages and moments of your journey and think about whether you could express that journey in song. Your song choice can be one you listened to during that time or one that speaks to that experience. When you use music to reflect on where you've been on your spiritual journey, you have a chance to find touchstones, or hearing cues, for those places in your life. Feeling down and out? Play a song from when your spirit was light and free. Want to get back to that time when you did a lot of wondering and questioning? Play the song you chose for that time in your life. Don't forget to keep adding to that playlist as time, and your journey with the Holy One, continues.

AND NOW FOR SOMETHING COMPLETELY DIFFERENT

In Zach Braff's 2004 movie *Garden State*, one of the most beautiful, talented actresses of our generation gets downright weird, and it's awesome. Natalie Portman plays Sam, a young woman who's an honest pathological liar and the love interest for Braff's character Andrew. Not long after the two meet, Sam and Andrew are getting to know each other at her house when she introduces him to one of her many eccentricities. Whenever she's feeling unoriginal, Sam does a strange dance or makes weird noises so she can feel unique again. In encouraging Andrew to give it a whirl, she insists, "it's refreshing, you should try it."

Who are we to argue with an Oscar winner (at least this Oscar winner's kooky character)? Not all of us are singers but we can make a joyful noise. Just start singing, or chanting, or making strange noises with a musical twist—just go for it! Relax and be ridiculous, be daring, be vulnerable. Let down your walls and release whatever music may be lurking inside you. Remember how we said some traditions say we all have an individual tune, a soul song? This *probably* isn't what was meant, but you never know! By letting yourself be open and silly, you're letting yourself connect to the creative flow of the universe. Just by being open to that flow through the medium of music, you may make some lovely—and maybe even needed—discoveries about your own creativity.

While you're making some joyful noise, pick up a musical instrument. Get yourself a tambourine, a keyboard, castanets, a djembe, bells, whatever! Now play. Let the sound that comes from your instrument find its own rhythm, its own path, its own direction. Go with that flow. Maybe you'll actually find a song pleasing to the ear—or maybe you'll make your dog cry out in pain. Don't worry about achieving some sort of musical harmony. Just play. Let the notes lead you into a place where perfection is not the point and only exploration matters. Embrace the creative freedom and let it lead you to the source of imagination. In the practice, in being a part of that creative endeavor—even if it doesn't seem "good"—you'll connect to that wonderful music of the heavens.

Once you've gotten comfortable just making musical noise, you may want to try a more focused approach. Singing your prayers is a time-honored tradition. While both of your authors are rooted in the Christian faith, we love the opportunity to attend services at a synagogue. Sure, we're suckers for the ritual and the Hebrew, but we're also enchanted by the cantor. She stands up there in front of the whole congregation and leads the people in sung prayer. As she sings the prayers, she both guides and inspires. The music is simple and stunning, the prayers profound and powerful.

> You're entering into play with the Creator of All Things Silly and Sublime.

You don't need a group of people to lead in order to explore sung prayer (in other words, don't start using your daily subway ride or time in the check-out line as a chance to have a captive audience to engage this particular practice). You don't need to have a song in mind before you start singing your prayer, nor do you need to have the words prepared. Open your mouth and let those words and the notes they attach themselves to flow forth. Don't be self-conscious; just sing. Pretend you're in a musical and the only way you can get your emotions or prayers out is to burst into song. On a slight tangent: have you ever spent a day as though you were in a musical? Or what about an opera—where *everything* is sung? *I'm going to cross the street! Oh heavens, this is me almost being run over by a car. Look both ways. Look both ways next time.* Yes, this definitely brings us back to the realm of ridiculousness that our Garden State-inspired prayer practice lives in. With these exercises, you're not just prepping for your upcoming improv audition, you're entering into play with the Creator of All Things Silly and Sublime. And, hey, once you've entered into musical land, breaking into sung prayer won't seem like a stretch at all!

Too much spontaneity for one moment (or day)? Find a prayer you like or write one down before you attempt to sing your prayers. Once you know the words you'd like to lift up in song, let the words find a note. What feels right, natural? Conversely, you can also take a tune you know—probably a simple one—and create new words to express what you'd like to lift up in song. Not feeling particularly creative, but want to connect to the musical prayers of the centuries anyway? Find a church's songbook, or

YouTube "psalm tunes" and try singing those prayers of the ancient Israelites—some of the tunes churches use are really easy. Let the music be the medium through which your spirit soars.

A ONE AND A TWO AND A...

Stretching your creative muscles isn't a necessity. Sometimes you'll want to sing or hear or play a prayer without having to create. Explore the vast gigabytes of music already created, music in which others in the past, right now, and even in the future know release and relief.

One musical style that doesn't get much radio time but has incredible transcendent power is jazz. A night out at a local jazz club isn't just filled with whatever spirit the bartender is serving. Reflecting on music and the spirit, saxophonist David Liebman (an NEA Jazz Masters lifetime achievement award winner and sideman to other greats, including Miles Davis) notes that both are abstracts—things you can neither see nor touch. When playing music, the fact that the spiritual self "lays in the same invisible realm puts the musician on that wavelength, whether they know it or not."[3]

Donald Miller's book *Blue Like Jazz*, and the movie of the same name, plays with the connection between jazz and the divine. In the book, Miller speaks of his struggle with jazz because it never resolves, and he compares that to his struggle with God—who also never resolves.[4] Finding a metaphor for the Holy in music works for us, though we connect with something a bit different than Miller. Jazz troubles some people because you can never be sure what you're going to get. A piece stays true to form but for some the improvisation is too much. Though not exactly random, it's not predictable—often for the listener *or* the musician. A piece can take you places you never thought you'd go—or even could go—until you do. If that doesn't sound like journeying with God, we don't know what does.

Get out an old jazz album—Coltrane's *A Love Supreme* is a particular favorite—and listen. Let waves of sound wash over you. Let yourself be carried away into that realm of imagination and possibility. Take note of whatever connection you may make between what you hear and your experience of the divine.

All that jazzed out? Consider engaging in music you may not be as familiar with. In the Burgundy region of France, there's a small town called Taizé. Near this small town is an ecumenical monastic community with

---

3. Quoted in Danielle Graham, "Spirituality in Jazz." *Superconsciousness*, April 15, 2012, http://www.superconsciousness.com/topics/art/spirituality-jazz.
4. Donald Miller, *Blue Like Jazz* (Nashville: Thomas Nelson, 2003), ix.

brothers from across the globe. They lead a simple, reflective life centered on promoting and praying for peace, unity, and reconciliation for all peoples. They also happen to be one of the hottest monastic communities around. If you were to drop by there on any given day, you'd probably see thousands of visitors who've come to spend a week in song, prayer, service, Bible study, and community-building. And most of these visitors would be young adults. There's something about the simplicity and the purpose that calls out to young adults from around the world, and it is reflected in the community's worship. No wonder in many religious communities the music from Taizé has become a staple for prayer.

The songs are simple to learn; a phrase or two is usually repeated over and over again. The use of this repetition invites you to get lost in the words and tune so you don't have to think so much; they melt away as your heart is engulfed in the majesty and mystery of God. For those of you who are musicians, think about what happens when you practice a piece over and over again. Once you've gotten past the "mastery" stage of your practice, you can enjoy the feel of the music coming forth from your instruments. Many musicians we know have a few songs they play to get warmed up, to center themselves in their craft. The music of Taizé can center you in the presence of the divine.[5]

Delve deeper into our musical heritage. The Renaissance period gave the world musicians whose works still resonate with listeners. Much music written during this time was performed in cathedrals and to the glory of God—along with the particular king or emperor in power at the time. The thoughtful pieces, the soaring voices, the harmonies invoke mystery and majesty. Interested in exploring this world? Go to iTunes or YouTube and search for names like Palestrina, William Byrd, Thomas Tallis, Hans Leo Hassler, Josquin des Prez, or Tomas Luis de Victoria. Sample some music; find a composer or a particular piece that seems to carry the voice of God's Spirit for you, and listen. Let yourself be taken away by the song. Sure, sing along if you can rock out the boy soprano sound. Otherwise, participate by offering your full attention.

Take a further step back into the history of sacred music, and you'll encounter plainsong. What's that, you non-music-majors ask? It's a form of music that only involves the voice—no maracas allowed. Words are sung in a free form (no clear meter the notes must obey) and include

---

5. Interested in learning more about this community? Go to their website: www.taize.fr and read up on the wonderful things they are doing—and how you might be able to visit. You can also hear some of their music as well as find the words and chords for songs on this site. You can also find a Taizé prayer podcast which will bring you song and scripture.

only a melody. The music is simple and haunting. The best-known style of plainsong is probably Gregorian chant—still used in certain churches today. Ever seen *Monty Python and the Holy Grail* (or the 2006 Broadway musical adaption *Spamalot*)? If the answer is yes, you know—or are at least familiar with—the form. The song the monks chant as they smack themselves in the head with their prayer books is Gregorian chant (though most chants don't include the self-inflicted beating!). Not a Python fan? You still may have been exposed to plainsong. If you were around and somewhat musically aware in the mid-90s, you may even own an old CD of chant. Though it was recorded in the 70s, the album *Chant* by the Benedictine Monks of Santo Domingo de Silos was re-released in 1994 and went triple platinum. Really. Triple platinum monks.

One of our favorite composers of plainsong hasn't ever gone triple platinum but she's amazing in her own right. Born in 1098, Hildegard started seeing visions at a young age—which would work well for her as she would soon be shipped off to a Benedictine monastery as her family's tithe of sorts to the church. She rose up the ranks and was unanimously voted abbess in 1136. During her life, Hildegard exchanged letters with kings and queens, defied religious authorities when their rules contradicted what she claimed to have heard directly from God, and wrote. A lot. She recorded her visions (which are both wonderful and wacky to read), wrote what's considered by some to be the first morality play, and composed hymn after beautiful hymn.

While there are no recordings from Hildegard's time (duh) and some of her music has lost the notes to accompany the lyrics, the medieval mystic still has some great albums out there. You can download her songs and buy sheet music for many of her chants.[6] Play a track and let the soaring voices break through the rush of the day and invite you to a place of peace. Sing out one of her chants, letting your voice join the melody sung over centuries. As you listen or sing, enter into an intimate conversation with the Holy. In exploring the musical expressions of faith of old, may you feel supported, sustained, and swept away into mystery.

REDUCE, REUSE, RECYCLE

What do Yankee Doodle, the theme to *Gilligan's Island*, and the Mickey Mouse march all have in common? You can sing the words of that well-known song Amazing Grace to any of those tunes. Go ahead, try it, we'll wait.

(Now good luck getting those out of your head!)

---

6. Hildegard Publishing Company is the place to go if you're interested in sheet music.

Why does that work? They all share the same meter, conveniently called "common meter." Songs that have the same meter can be interchanged— you can use the lyrics of one on the tune of another and vice versa. Other than being a cool fact, why does anyone care about this? For those of you who have had exposure to hymns as a child, you may have a few old favorites. In working with folks our age, we've found that songs like *Be Thou My Vision* and *On Eagles' Wings* hold meaning even for people who no longer affiliate themselves with institutional religion. There's something about these hymns that resonates with us. We'll sing *Come Thou Fount of Every Blessing*, even though most of us don't have a clue what that Ebenezer is we're raising in the second verse.[7]

Take an old hymn or spiritual song for which you have a fondness. What about that song speaks to you? Is it the words? The tune? Both? Experiment with changing some things around. What would happen if you wrote new or adapted lyrics to your hymn tune? Hymnists do it all the time and the changes can be powerful. In fact, just recently one of your intrepid authors undertook to write new words for the old hymn "Leaning On The Everlasting Arms"—words that specifically spoke to the spiritual community that would be singing them together:

> "Here among these friends, truth we dare to speak, leaning on the everlasting arms.
> Courage we will find, as your way we seek, leaning on the everlasting arms."[8]

Or, for example, the writer John Bell took the words of Psalm 40 and put them to that good old Amazing Grace tune. You can also take the words you know and love and see if there are any other tunes that will support those words. Think back on *Amazing Grace*. Think about *House of the Rising Sun* by the Animals and then lay the words of the hymn on top of that tune: you've just layered famous words of grace over well-known sounds of brokenness.

If you're intrigued by playing with songs of old, consider having fun with the psalms. Psalms, you say? Yup, the psalms; they are songs, after all! While the original musical notations have been lost to time, plenty of people have added their two cents, or two bars if you will, to the poems. Take one of the psalms and add accompaniment to it. You don't have to have a whole complicated composition. Try just putting a rhythm to the

---

7. "Here I raise my Ebenezer, hither by thy help I've come." No, you're not claiming to be lifting up that old curmudgeon who hangs out with ghosts. It's some sort of item that reminds you of God's presence—literally meaning a stone of help. The phrase comes from a story in 1 Samuel 7.
8. Teri Peterson, January 2012.

piece to start. Discover the natural meter and play with it. Then if you'd like to go for the advanced degree, give the beats specific notes and see what happens.

Just like with hymns, you can also take the psalms and play around with the words. Rewrite them to reflect your own experiences and language. Borrowing from ancient songs and putting your own spin on it is not plagiarism (at least if you don't try to sell said song) but a spiritual practice whose practitioners include Mary, the Mother of God. Her song (commonly called the *Magnificat*) borrows heavily from the prayer of another awesome woman—Hannah.[9] One of our favorite examples of a modern twist is by Rob Lacey from his book *Word on the Street*—a retelling of the much of the bible. A classic English translation of Psalm 23 begins "The Lord is my Shepherd, I shall not want. He makes me lie down in green pastures; he leads me beside still waters; he restores my soul." Lacey's words read: "You're my guide and my guard, my minder, my mentor. What more do I need? What's better at the centre? You sit me down, put my best CD on, and my soul remembers who I am again."[10] Find a psalm that may be particularly meaningful (Psalm 1, 8, 13, 121, 139 would all be good places to start) and play with the words. Make it your own.

> "I think music always has the power to change, heal, bring understanding and bring people together."
> —ICE CUBE[11]

People in areas ranging from medicine to horticulture to art agree: music is powerful. It can stir up buried feelings, inspire growth, promote healing, drive creativity, bridge gaps, and invoke the Holy. No matter how musically inclined you may or may not be, how can you not want to see what this medium might offer for your spiritual life? Singing pretty, singing plain, composing or just going a bit crazy with noise: engage music in any way and you may encounter the divine. Be it punk or polka, reggae or rock, listen to notes, get lost in the lyrics, and be open to what music has to offer. By entering into the song (be it your soul song, the universe's song, or just a good new single) you may meet the Source of song. Go. Make some beautiful music.

---

9. Compare Mary's words found in Luke chapter 1 to Hannah's found in 1 Samuel chapter 2.
10. Rob Lacey, *Word on the Street* (Grand Rapids: Zondervan, 2003), 149.
11. Rob Markham. "Ice Cube Reflects On The Power of Music, 20 Years After L.A. Riots." *MTV News*, April 30, 2012, www.mtv.com/news/articles/1684169/los-angeles-riots-20th-anniversary-ice-cube.jhtml.

GOING TO PRACTICE

Explore the raw power of a beat. Pick a rather mundane activity you do, a chore, an exercise regimen, or something as basic as showering, and add a little dubstep. The fast-tempo, bass infused music (which can be heard as of this book's publication on dance floors and spinning classes across the world) will get your blood pumping and help you zone in on what you're doing. From runners to writers, people have found a motivating rhythm in this genre. Take this time to be led by the beat. Let the music influence your own internal tempo.

SEE MORE...

Don Saliers and Emily Saliers, *A Song to Sing, A Life to Live: Reflections on Music as Spiritual Practice* (San Francisco: Jossey-Bass, 2005).

FIVE

~~~~

MAKING IT UP AS WE GO

*"To commemorate a past event, you kill and eat
an animal. It's a ritual sacrifice, with pie."*
—ANYA, DISCUSSING THANKSGIVING[1]

The word "ritual" has gotten kind of a bad rap in our culture. For many of us, it brings to mind one of three things: something meaningless and rote, repeated just because it's what you're supposed to do but you're not sure why; something people suffering with Obsessive-Compulsive Disorder do; some kind of cult practice with blood and bones and Kool-Aid. Hearing the word can bring up mental images of people kneeling and saying the same words over and over every week, or of people gathered around a symbol chanting but not knowing what they're really doing. These associations contribute to our cultural sense that rituals are "devoid of meaning," and it's better to always be in the moment, to make things up as we go, to do what feels right and forget about creating traditions that will just end up bogging us down in boredom.

If this is all ritual is—either a symptom of a mental disorder, a pointless exercise in living in the past, or a frightening foray into the supernatural, then it's right for us to abandon the idea of ritual. We want to feel, and to feel deeply. We want to be engaged with our minds, our spirits, and our bodies, not just going through the motions somebody hundreds of years ago made up. But here's the twist in our narrative: "ritual" is not necessarily synonymous with "rote." It is possible for us to engage in rituals, and even

---

1. *Buffy the Vampire Slayer*, "Pangs," (episode 64, season 4.8), originally aired October 19, 1999.

to create our own, as a way of organizing and making meaning out of our life experiences.

The thing is, ritual is an important part of life. We may not always call it that, but it happens nonetheless. For instance, many families have traditions surrounding holidays—when to hang Christmas stockings, when to open presents, what to say around the Thanksgiving table (hint: you'll probably want to avoid mentioning ritual sacrifice), what to do on birthdays. Those are all rituals—actions we do to make meaning, organize experiences into something that makes sense, and mark important occasions. When we sit around the table and say one thing we're grateful for, that's a ritual—one with deep meaning for many people. When we open one present on Christmas Eve and save the rest for Christmas morning, that's a ritual that helps us remember (even in the midst of the consumerism of the Christmas season) that a little delayed gratification and anticipation can be a good thing.

> Whatever we call it, ritual is an important part of life.

Our lives as young adults are marked by any number of experiences that could really use new rituals to help us as we sort out what life means and what it looks like in our new context. The church and culture have plenty of rituals for what becoming an adult used to look like—weddings, house blessings, baptisms. But getting married, buying a house, and starting a family are not the regular rites of passage for 22-year-olds that they used to be. As we spend more time on education, go into more debt, and work more but earn less, many of us are delaying marriage, can't afford a house or kids, and find ourselves looking for the new transition-to-adulthood markers.

The new normal for young adults often involves regularly changing jobs, by choice or as victims of the economy. We move frequently—whether to cheaper apartments or to new towns as our jobs move or disappear or as our relationships change. Our romances don't lead inevitably to marriage the way they did for many of our parents and grandparents, so breakups are a regular part of life. Even our holidays may be spent with our found-families—friends and neighbors—rather than our families of origin, because of distance or economics or the realities of juggling work and divorced families.

How do we make sense of these life experiences when we're busy blazing the trail? How do we organize our hopes, dreams, fears, realities, loves, losses, and find a sense of the Holy in the midst of them? How do we mark these life events that don't have rituals already attached to them the way marriage or kids do? To just ignore the importance of these moments doesn't make them go away—it only leaves them hanging, waiting for a therapist to help us sort them out later. While that may still be necessary, we believe there is a way to create ritual that makes meaning out of the lives we live now, as twenty-first–century young adults. But the ways we can make meaning out of our lives aren't going to be handed down to us; we'll have to make it up as we go. And that's okay.

Recently, I (Teri) had a really bad year. And I do mean a bad year—work was insane and awful on every level, my friends were driving me crazy, I didn't know what to do with myself, my family was needy even from thousands of miles away, and I wasn't sure I could take it anymore. When that nightmare finally came to an end—or at least looked like it was going to get a little more manageable—a friend and I decided to mark that year and put it behind us. But we needed a way to do it that wasn't cheesy. We decided to create a ritual that we could do at the beginning of every year, to help us refocus and move forward. I call it the "putting the past in the past" ritual. It goes like this: we build a fire in the fire pit outside. We drink some wine. We write down everything we can remember from the past year that didn't go well—every irritating person, every frustrating encounter, every drama, every unfulfilled hope, every nightmare lived out, every failure. When we finally finish with the list (for that first year, it took a long time), we talk over our lists, airing the badness one last time. Then we put the paper in the fire, and watch it burn. Then we roast marshmallows over the fire, reminding ourselves that something sweet can come out of the bitterness of the past, if we just let go and move forward. We make s'mores and laugh well into the night.

Often when I tell people my parents' or grandparents' age about this ritual, they tease me for being so sentimental. The thing is, it works. I put the anger and frustration of the past year into the fire and commit myself to bringing something good out of those ashes. Sure, I could just tell myself I'm going to get over it and move on, but there's something about the physicality of the ritual, the sharing of the pain, and tasting the new life ahead.[2] It's a way of marking time, admitting failure and hurts, and moving forward. It helps hold us accountable to one another and to ourselves

---

2. In many ways, this is what communion is about! We admit our failings, we proclaim that we cannot do this alone, and we come to the table to taste and see that God is good—and this feast is our strength for the journey. But even when your communion bread is amazing, it's not as tasty as s'mores!

even as it reminds us that we cannot change the past but we still have hope for the future. I can also imagine doing something similar in the face of a failure—whether personal or professional. It would be a way of acknowledging that I didn't get it right, and things didn't go as planned, but there's a new thing coming and I need to be open to it.

We spent a lot of time—probably 2 months—talking about what this ritual should be like. We went through a lot of ideas before we settled on this one. Part of the beauty of the ritual is that we made it up for ourselves, so it would speak to us and our lives in this place and time. True, we built it on ancient traditions like confession and communion, but the way we did it was 100% us. It may not work for everyone; it may not even work for us forever. But we feel confident that everyone can create something similar that would help to make meaning out of the experience of life. Sometimes life is hard, sometimes it's frustrating, sometimes it doesn't go according to plan, sometimes it leaves us with a bitter taste in our mouths. Finding ways to express that, to give it voice and bring it out into the open, is important. Some of us may come from religious, family, or community traditions where we already have rituals for this kind of thing—such as confession and penance or other forms of mutual accountability. Others of us will have to make something up so that we can grow through the experience and move toward a better future.

One of the beauties of growing up in our time is the space for creativity. It's almost expected that we'll think outside the box and look for new ways of being and doing. Yet we also yearn for consistency, for a tradition meaty enough that we can really grab on and make it our own, something to which we can anchor ourselves. Without those traditions, we often feel adrift in a chaotic sea of unlimited opportunity. Particularly as many of us have a hard time connecting to religious rituals *and* are simultaneously far from family and those traditions, it's important to make space for creating new ritual in the midst of our lives.

FRIENDS AND FEASTING

We're not here to tell you what to do, we're here to spark conversation and ideas in your own community. Only you can draw on your faith background and your current context to create the ritual that will speak to you, your time, your life, your place. So here are a few things we've done with our friends—may they ignite your own creativity!

One of the things many of us like to do is have friends over for a meal— as we gather around the table, we can share food and laughter and stories. Getting together to eat is a profoundly biblical practice—offering and accepting hospitality, sharing meals, building community around the table. It's also part of our calling to make the world a better place, and many of us are interested in how we can be connected to our global family. Perhaps a ritual for get-togethers with friends is in order. You could have a map in your dining room and mark where all the food for the meal came from, as a reminder of how interconnected we are in our global community, and then give thanks around the table for those who produce and transport and prepare the food you're about to enjoy together. If you have a potluck, have everyone who brings a dish also bring a print-out about the country or state (or local farmer!) the main ingredient comes from, so you can learn more about the world that feeds us. You could have a ritual similar to one that many of us participate in at Thanksgiving, where each person around the table offers something—whether it's something they're grateful for, a story, a joke, or a piece of good news. You might create a ritual together as a group, including elements from each person's family. Creating together is one of the best ways to build community, so gather for dinner and ask around—what would be meaningful to people you hang out with?

When I (Amy) first moved to the little Virginia town I now call home, I didn't know a soul. I moved from a big city with plenty of things to do and lots of friends to a small town with no Starbucks and not one person I could instantly call up to go to the movies. Not too long after moving to town, I started meeting people and finding folks to go to see the newest blockbuster with, but it took months to meet and make friends that would become my new family.

How'd I meet/make these friends? It involves Easter and good bit of food. I met another young twenty-something who had recently moved to the same small town on account of her husband's schooling. We were both experiencing holidays away from our families and good friends. While Easter has never been a big holiday for my family, it was for hers. She came up with an idea and I grasped on to it. We would have a huge open house potluck Easter Sunday, invite all the young adults we knew, and encourage them to invite all the young adults they knew.

We made a Facebook event, rented a few tables and chairs for all the people we hoped would come, and waited. Apparently, if you provide food and libations, they will indeed come. Throughout the day, people brought food and feasted and, as often happens over a meal, laughed and created community. I made new friends that day and got to know casual acquaintances even better. Something even more surprising happened—a tradition was born.

Though my friend who plotted the first potluck with me has moved away, our event happens every year. Friends gather together and cast the net of welcome wide, inviting all to the event we now call "Easter Feaster." People who aren't even a bit religious say it's their favorite holiday. Why? Perhaps because of all the good food and drink to share. Perhaps they love what I love, the wide assortment of people who gather and share stories over a meal.

I don't know what will happen when I move away from this small town I now joyfully call home. I'd like to think I'll take Easter Feaster with me. It has become integral to how I make meaning out of Easter. I celebrate the resurrection of Jesus by creating community over a meal. Like many rituals, this one may only feel right for this place and these people. Whatever happens in the future, I'm loving it now.

WHEN LIFE GIVES YOU A LEMON...

Moving away is a common experience in our culture these days. It's not unusual for someone to move for a job, for family reasons, or for school. It's always hard when a friend moves away. A ritual to mark the end of a season in the life of your friend-group is a way to mark the experiences you've had together and prepare for a new page in the book of your friendship. When one of my (Teri's) friends moved away recently, we decided to have a backwards party. We didn't want this to be the *end* of anything, and "goodbye" was completely out of the question, so we decided to run the whole party in reverse. We greeted each other with "bye!" and then proceeded to have drinks, then dessert, then a board game, then dinner, then a round of appetizers, and we ended with "hello!" as we left. It was a way to remember that our relationship isn't ending, just changing.

Another of our friends has a birthday tradition they call a candle ceremony, and it is easily adapted for moving-away moments. Everyone in the room has a lighted candle in front of them (obviously this works best in the dark!). When everyone is gathered, someone begins by telling a story about the person being celebrated, or saying something for which they are grateful about that person. When they're finished, they place the candle in front of the person who is leaving. This continues until everyone has spoken and all the candles are gathered in front of the one person. It's a beautiful way to appreciate someone, and to physically surround them with the light of the community—as they go, they take our prayers, our light, our love with them into the new place, so they do not go alone.

Sometimes the experiences we have in life are less easy to figure out how to ritualize—for instance, breakups happen all the time and our dating lives are complicated, not always going the way we hope. Some of the rituals we've seen in many a movie montage, like cutting the ex out of the pictures or burning the love letters, are harder to do in the digital age. Sure, you could Photoshop your ex out of all those pictures, but dang it takes a long time! You could print pictures and cut them up, but that's expensive and not particularly tree-friendly. You could just trash all the photos, but you probably want at least some memories of visiting a place, or maybe it's a good picture of you. And yeah, you can delete the emails and de-friend or un-follow them, but somehow that's a lot less satisfying than cutting and burning. Plus we all know that nothing is ever truly gone from the internet. So what do we do to mark those transitions of relationship, from single to couple to single—often repeatedly—in our young adult years? And what about those long-term relationships, or even marriages, that end? There are plenty of rituals for making relationships— from dating norms to weddings to anniversary celebrations. But ending relationships? Whether it's a bad breakup or an amicable one, and whether it's the end of a romantic relationship or a friendship, we need new ways of moving through that pain and loss and into a new way of being. We need to find ways to re-center ourselves in the One whose name is Love.

> We need to find ways to re-center ourselves in the One whose name is Love.

The ritual you might create to mark the ending of a relationship will be specific to who you are and what kind of situation it was. Maybe you want to do something like the past-is-past ritual complete with bonfire like the one we described a few pages ago. Maybe the idea of photo-shopping your ex out of dozens or hundreds of digital photos sounds cathartic. Or if that is really too much work, get yourself a box and stuff all your relationship mementos in it. Put it next to your bed. The next day, move it further away from your space. The next day, even further. Keep moving it away until eventually it meets the garbage, attic, or closet of no return. Not into something so symbolic? Maybe you just want to find a way to mark a new chapter in your life by taking on something new. A new hobby, a new haircut, heck, even a new city. Anything that helps you move on. Maybe you have that break-up movie or cd, the one you turn to when life sucks, as a reminder that it doesn't always feel so bad.

If you need to process with people, perhaps you'll want to gather with some friends and make lists of all the reasons you are awesome and love-able, as a reminder to you that you are a beloved child of God and quite the catch. Or, if you need to be reminded why that ex of yours is no loss, you and your friends can even make a list of the ways in which he or she is a bullet dodged. That second list may not sound very holy but it can be quite cathartic. It can also lead to a moment of grace. After you've made a list of his or her negative qualities add the phrase "loved by God." Even when we need to let people go from our lives we can entrust them to the love of God. If we have no personal love to share with someone, we can still allow God's love to have the last word. A bit of advice: hold onto that first list for however long you'd like but toss the second soon after making it. (The writing's liberating but holding on is unhealthy).

Maybe lists aren't your thing. Maybe a comfort-food-potluck is in order. Maybe it's time for a pick-up-and-break-up party, where everyone comes with their funniest (in retrospect, of course) breakup stories and worst pick-up lines and acts them out like charades. Or perhaps what you really need is the chance to just be real, to be heartbroken, to be hurt. A gathering of friends who can be safe (not judgmental, not inappropriately humorous), where you just spill your hopes and dreams that won't come true this time, where you can cry or rage or whatever, and a ritual to mark that loss—perhaps lighting a candle for each dashed hope, or naming fears for the future—might be just what you need. We often think that grief is only related to death, but we grieve many things, including broken rela-tionships, lost friends, lost jobs—and often those are related to the sense of a lost future. Finding a way to name that loss and release that version of your future (preferably without releasing balloons into the sky as they inevitably come back down and can end up in some poor, hungry animal's stomach!) will help you be open to the new future unfolding.

Once you've been able to be authentic and vulnerable you can spend some time with the things you're going to want to keep. Things you're go-ing to want to hold onto in the future. We don't mean the baseball caps she bought you or the ticket stubs from concerts he took you to. We're talking about the ways you've grown and the things you've learned and even the funny stories you may want to tell again once the pain of disappointment has died down. Pick up an aloe plant at your local garden center and place it somewhere in your living space. Let this serve as a reminder of growth and healing.

All these ways of marking transitions in our lives are things we have made up over the past few years. They have helped us as our lives have changed, as the economy or family or other circumstances have moved us geographically or emotionally. They've given us a way to grieve and a way to celebrate, a way to let go and a way to move forward. There are thousands of ways to mark these moments—the key is to create something that works for you and your community. Maybe burning your frustrations isn't the way forward for you, or maybe you only eat out with your friends, not at your homes, or maybe you live in a place where it's more common for new people to move in than for people to move away. Whatever the circumstance, with a little creative thinking and an eye toward building a community through shared experience, you too can create a ritual that will help make life more meaningful and holy for you.

GOING TO PRACTICE
Get some friends together and create a ritual—silly or serious—that you might want to do every time you hang out. It doesn't need to be long or involved; it could be as simple as a secret handshake or a particular greeting, or as creative and complex as you want! Figure out what works for your group and let that ritual help you deepen your relationships with each other and with the Holy.

SEE MORE...
Herbert Anderson and Edward Foley, *Mighty Stories, Dangerous Rituals: Weaving Together the Human and the Divine* (San Francisco: Jossey-Bass, 1998).

SIX

COME TOGETHER

*"My ongoing struggle against the Capitol,
which has so often felt like a solitary journey,
has not been undertaken alone."* —KATNISS[1]

Belonging is one of the key needs of a human being.[2] We're hard-wired for community, and we want to fit in, to feel valued and loved. That's one of the reasons middle school is so hard: everyone feels like an outcast at some point or another, when all we want is a group of friends to help us figure out who the heck we are! Too often that experience continues beyond our school days and it feels like we're on our own in the world. We're told to stand on our own two feet, make our own way, be independent.

With the instant communication now available, we are finally realizing that our independence is more of an illusion than we would like to think. We depend on other people, and on a relationship between people and the earth. The web of creation includes not just the air moved by a butterfly flapping its wings in one part of the world, but all the ways we interact. For instance, verbal violence (intentional or unintentional) can affect people we've never met—when we speak a harsh word to another, particularly a

---

1. Suzanne Collins, *Mockingjay* (Scholastic Press: New York, 2010), 90.
2. "A need to belong, that is, a need to form and maintain at least a minimum quantity of interpersonal relationships, is innately prepared (and hence nearly universal) among human beings." Roy F. Baumeister and Mark R. Leary, "The Need to Belong: Desire for Interpersonal Attachments as a Fundamental Human Motivation," *Psychological Bulletin*, 117, no.3 (1995): 499. Another, more accessible, conversation about this concept is in Diana Butler Bass's book, *Christianity After Religion* (New York: HarperOne, 2012), especially in chapter 6.

child, they often pass that anger on to others and the cycle can be very difficult to break. Hospitality offered to one person can also echo across time and space as people "pay it forward." The ways we interact with each other matter—not just to the relationship itself, not just to our personal psyche, but to all the other strands that connect us.

This interdependence is not only apparent in our marketplace and political lives, but in our spiritual lives as well. How we engage with what the Spirit is doing within us and through us is an important question that affects the way we live in the world. Since we are definitely not advocating for being isolated from the world, why would we want a spirituality that is disconnected from the web of creation, people, or society?

> "Everybody is a story.
> When I was a child, people sat around kitchen tables and told their stories. ...
> It is the way the wisdom gets passed along.
> The stuff that helps us to live a life worth remembering."
>
> —DR. RACHEL NAOMI REMEN[3]

Spirituality is often considered an intensely private matter—I do my thing, you do yours, we don't talk about it, and it's all good. Particularly with the way the First Amendment has been popularly understood, we are shy about sharing our spiritual lives with others. We hear a lot about being spiritual, but the notion is often vague when divorced from community. It ends up being just a conglomeration of things that make us feel good about ourselves, or pump up our energy for a day or two. This isolated spirituality also lends itself to narcissism. We end up so involved with ourselves and how we feel today that we forget that we're hardly the first people to seek a spiritual experience and that it's not really *all* about us, after all. Seeking a spiritual life needs to be a balance between feeding ourselves and participating in the world.

If we pursue a spiritual path only as individuals, we miss out on amazing opportunities for growth, and we also run the risk of doing something "for God" that lands us in the lead spot on the six o'clock news. One of the gifts the Abrahamic faiths offer us is the acknowledgment that we cannot seek God in a vacuum, nor can we discern God's call solely on our own. We need a community to listen with us, to seek together, to offer accountability and encouragement.

---

3. Rachel Naomi Remen, *Kitchen Table Wisdom: Stories That Heal* (New York: Riverhead, 1996), xxvii.

Some of us find that community through church, synagogue, temple, or mosque. Others of us may find that community at the local coffee shop, in a group of friends, at school or work, or at book group. What matters is not really the *where* or even the *how* of the community. Far more important is that it is a group of people that looks for the meaning behind our experience and that supports and challenges each other in the living of this life.

Established faith communities also offer something we rarely experience in our world anymore: intergenerational relationship. So often our relationships with those older and younger are limited to familial or instructional ties; we hardly ever get to develop friendships with people of different generations. We grow up surrounded by 30 people of the same age, with just one or two adults from outside our family. In a church, though, there are people from 0-100 all sitting in the same room. While we're not fans of the patronizing "when I was your age" comments, it's still true that we can learn a lot from hearing the stories of those who lived through the Great Depression or a series of World Wars. We can also learn a lot by sharing with those younger than we are our stories of watching the Challenger explosion in our first grade classroom, or what we remember of traveling before 9/11.

Growing up far away from any extended family, Amy rarely had the experience of sitting in the pews with her grandparents. The memories she has of holding her grandmother's hand during prayers and watching her grandfather clearly *not* sing during the hymns are some of her favorites. It wasn't until she was serving in her first call as a pastor that she understood why those memories were so dear. Every Sunday morning worshippers would come up to the front of the church and gather around the communion table. Families would usually stand together as the congregation made a circle around the feast of the Lord's Supper. One pair stood apart from the rest. A blond, cherubic little girl who, as soon as she could walk, would come stand next to an older, sweet and sassy grandmother. The pair would hold hands as they waited for the bread and the cup. What made these two particularly meaningful to Amy is that the older woman was not actually this girl's grandmother. The little girl would walk up to the front of the church with her parents and grandparents then leave their side to go hold this other woman's hand. Every week.

Every week this brought tears to Amy's eyes. This is what the memories of worshipping with her own grandparents hinted at. This is what community is about. It reaches past ages, bloodlines, cultures, and languages to something more precious.

Our spirits can be lifted by singing alongside someone who can no longer read the notes but sings from memory with gusto. Our prayer lives can be enhanced by praying for those sitting across the room, and knowing they are praying for us. Our common hope can be bolstered when a group of us stand in solidarity with people in other lands even as we stumble over the words of a prayer in a foreign language. In a faith community, we are reminded that we do not seek alone, and what we seek is not about us but about the transformation of the world.

Many of us have learned the hard way that religious communities are just as flawed as the human beings who belong to them. Some are more about belonging to the club than they are about seeking God. Some are single-issue communities, and if that issue is not your passion, then you won't fit in. Each community has its particular character or ethos, and it can be tricky to find a vibe that complements yours. And, of course, there are many communities where the hard aspects of life are glossed over in favor of easy answers, so people rarely share the deep struggles or pain, rarely know enough about each other to be encouraging or to hold one another accountable. Finding a community that is authentic and a good fit for your personality can feel like a daunting task. Churches and other faith groups are not perfect, nor do most of them claim to be. We might even go so far as to suggest that if a group *does* claim to be perfect, sinless, or otherwise too good to be true, you should back away slowly and look for a place where normal human beings can go through the ups and downs of life together.

> It is not good for people to be alone.

Having said that, the imperfection of community is not an excuse to avoid it altogether. Most of us have experienced real tension, or even dysfunction, in a group or a family, and yet we rarely respond by becoming hermits. It is not good for people to be alone. The occasional silent retreat or night at home with the dog? Sure. But walking this path of life, especially if you are trying to follow the way of Jesus, can't be done in isolation. We need each other as we navigate the complex web of life straddling the realities of our world and God's kingdom.

How do you find, or create, a community that will help you as you walk through life as a seeker of the sacred? How do you discover a group that both fits your needs and allows your gifts to flourish, a group that needs you as much as you need it? Or if you're already involved in a community, how do you continue to engage a deeper spiritual reality?

If you're looking for a place to start, there's always the first place we look for just about everything: the Internet. Look around at the faith groups in your area and do a little research, both on the local group and on any national body or denomination they belong to. Pick a couple and try them out. Remember that one visit is rarely enough to gauge a community, any more than one conversation is enough to understand a person. Try to meet some people while you're there. Check out how people interact with one another. Notice whether you click with the leadership. Look for a place that welcomes you as you are, and is willing to walk with you through the seeking. Look for a place where you can be nurtured and where you are offered opportunities to serve.

If none of those local congregations fit the bill, look for a Meetup group, a group that meets in a local bookstore or library, or a service organization that has regular meetings. There are lots of options out there for getting together with people—the trick is to find one that isn't just about reading the latest novel but is about growing relationships and exploring life together.

CHANGING IT UP

You may already belong to a group of one kind or another, whether it's roller derby, a church, or friends who watch football on Sunday afternoons. Not all these groups—including the churches!—are engaging the spiritual realm. But almost any group can be a spiritual community if that's what we're looking for. It can be as simple as talking about questions together. Often this perspective change begins with sharing our lives beyond "how's it going?" "Fine." When we were in seminary, our international student friends noted the strangeness of this customary exchange. Do I really want to know how you are? Usually not. Are we all always fine? Not likely. Why do we use these disingenuous words to say "hello"? Instead of this standard greeting, try asking questions like "what's been interesting in your life lately?" or "have you seen anything that moved your spirit this week?"

> "It won't matter what happens to us as long as we stay honest and accepting of each other's flaws and virtues."
>
> —ABED, ADDRESSING UNCERTAINTY, ON COMMUNITY[4]

In other words, go beyond just the superficial greeting and find ways to get into real conversation about real life. Being honest about the things we wonder about, the questions we have, the struggles we face, is the first step toward a deeper community.

---

4. *Community*, "Remedial Chaos Theory," (episode 52, season 3.4), originally aired October 12, 2011.

Some groups are not safe enough to go to this place. If that's the case in your groups, look for ways to shift that culture to one that values each person enough to let them be real, even if it makes others squirm a little. Real life is messy. We should be able to share that with each other.

This starts by simply looking at the people around you. Go ahead, look. In this moment, don't think of them by their name or as your child or spouse or friend—see them as a child of God. We can never be in true community without a perspective that begins with the other person's inherent worth as a human being. Once you have practiced this kind of vision, look for opportunities to encourage it in conversation. Someone say something profound? Admire it without sarcasm. Someone do something dumb? Focus on the action's problem, not the person's problem. Find ways to be genuinely positive about each person and their gifts, talents, and beauty. You don't have to always say "you're such a beloved child of God!" but that can be the subtext behind your words and actions.

When we see each other as people created in God's image, it becomes easier to ask questions that get at the real problem behind a situation, or to ponder big issues together. Don't be afraid to occasionally throw out a conversation topic you've never discussed before and see where it takes you.

Once a group has shifted into an encouraging and authentic personality, you might try looking at a sacred text together. Even if it's just a line of scripture followed by "what do you think that means?" or a discussion about something you saw on The History Channel that leads to a conversation about how we interpret the Bible, it's a point of entry to looking at what God is doing. We understand that some groups may fit more easily into this model than others. Don't force something that isn't there, but don't be afraid to nudge your friends toward a deeper relationship both within the group and with God.

As a way to foster deep connection and accountability, your group, or a group within your church, might consider writing individual "mission statements." Yes, mission statements are usually business practice, but they're also a way for each of us to think deeply about who we think God calls us to be, what our values and dreams are, and how we live in the world. Share these with each other, and then commit to asking one another how *that's* going, rather than just the generic "how are you?" When you see someone behaving in ways that are inconsistent with their mission statement, you know something's up and you can ask about it. Of course, this practice requires that we have enough trust to hear from one another without being immediately defensive. Sharing ourselves in this way can be very vulnerable, and it's a gift we offer to one another. A group practicing faithfulness in this way can also ask each other clarifying questions and be friendly voices as we seek a Spirit-led shape to our lives.

One model for such a group can be found in the Iona Community.[5] They are a "dispersed community," meaning that members do not necessarily live together. Instead they are bound by a common "rule of life" to which each member commits. Part of that rule is that members agree to meet together regularly in just the kind of group we're talking about now. They call them "family groups." In family group meetings, people share what's happening in their lives, they pray for one another, and they discuss how they're doing at keeping the rule. That means asking each other hard questions about how they spend time and money, the state of their spiritual lives, and the ways they put their beliefs and convictions into action. These family group meetings are an opportunity to grow as individuals even as friendships deepen. They are also a way to be intentional about the spiritual journey, recognizing that we can't do it on our own. It's like having someone check in with you about your mission statement every month. Of course, there's also some fun and food and laughter, too!

STARTING FROM SCRATCH

Can't find an established spiritual community that works for you, or been burned one too many times? Consider creating something new. Get a few friends together and talk about your hopes and dreams, your struggles and sorrows. If there's a younger clergy person in your area, maybe pull him or her into the conversation too—they have background many of us lack, and sometimes they have resources that can help us as we think things through. You'll want to think about at least some of these things:

- ❧ What kind of community do you wish you were a part of?
- ❧ What would help you as you grow into the person God created you to be?
- ❧ What is the purpose of gathering together?
- ❧ What do you want to learn? How will you explore together?
- ❧ Will there be ground rules for communication, accountability, and encouragement?
- ❧ Where will you meet?
- ❧ How will you invite people to join in?
- ❧ How do you want to serve?
- ❧ What passions or skills would you have to offer? (Often the gifts of a group of people is a great indicator of their calling. Have a lot of people who love teaching? Maybe you can be part of an after-school

---

5. Learn more at http://www.iona.org.uk.

program. Several of you with musical or poetic talent? Find a way to offer a free coffee-house/open-mic evening. You get the idea.)

✣ What do you sense the Spirit is doing that you want to be a part of?

That last question may be the most important. Amy recently participated in the formation of a new spiritual community and discovered how the Spirit was already out there, doing her thing, waiting for others to join. In a small town where bright, artistic young adults often found themselves standing still, searching for their muse or for connection, the Spirit was working to create a community where such searchers might gather to find meaning and purpose together. In listening to people's stories, those looking to form community found connections. Almost all it took was offering a gathering space and writers, musicians, students, activists, and other mystery chasers came together around cooking, conversation, and communion. While this may not always be the case, it was Amy's experience that discerning and then joining the Spirit's movement led to beautiful community. Where before there were isolated individuals with the desire to make an impact, now there is a welcoming community growing and giving.

Once you have a group together, we recommend creating a gathering ritual that will set the time apart for you. Maybe you'll light a candle. Maybe you'll sing a song, give each other high-fives, or share a moment you experienced the Divine today. Something that calls you together as a community seeking something more, walking through life with a different set of lenses. Use your time together to ask what God is doing in your lives, in your group, and in the world. Look intently and wonder about the mystery behind our understanding of reality. Use your new perspective to be a part of changing the world.

If you're looking for ideas, you might want to start by trying out some of the practices in this book together. There are ideas here for individuals and groups, and nearly everything can be adapted for different spaces and different size groups.

Remember that "to everything there is a season." It's possible that the community you form now will morph and shift, or maybe even come to an end. People move, grow apart, and need different things at different times. Engage fully now, find ways to encourage each other to be living good news, and don't assume you've failed if you don't end up starting the next mega-church or multi-million-dollar sensation. If the season for this community comes to an end, be sure to create a ritual celebrating the things the Spirit did in your midst and moving on to follow her in new directions. Be open to possibilities.

WORTH THE EFFORT

Still uncertain about this whole community thing? We understand. Teri grew up in a family that not only did *not* go to church, but was actively hostile to the idea of faith, organized religion, or a spirituality beyond science, philosophy, and the baseball field. The idea of setting foot in a church was as far from her mind as you can imagine. When the Spirit finally did nudge her through the doors as a young adult, it was for a concert, not for some big spiritual moment. What brought her back was the sense that together, we could make a big difference in the world. Through serving with others in a soup kitchen and a tutoring program, she ended up with that big spiritual moment—or, rather, a series of small spiritual moments that led up to a realization that she couldn't walk this journey alone. Sure, the hymns all say that God promises never to leave us, but the reality is that sometimes you need a tangible relationship if you're going to make it through life.

That doesn't mean it was easy. She went through the excitement of finding people who were asking the same questions and the wonder of exploring the faith tradition, through the disillusionment that comes with seeing the behind-the-scenes reality, and right on to the hard work of going through conflict. That last is really hard, because we have this idea that conflict means everything is falling apart, or we don't belong if we disagree. Sure, there are some disagreements that may be deal-breakers. But more often than not, conflict is an opportunity for us to grow. Just because something is difficult doesn't mean it's not worth doing! We have to learn to listen compassionately, express ourselves clearly, and seek God's Spirit *together*.[6] When we're part of a body, we don't get to just fly off on our own—we have to look for how our calling fits into a larger picture. It can be super frustrating, and it goes against the grain in so many ways, but it's also part of living in the kingdom of God while living in the world.

> When we gather into loving community, we are offered a glimpse at the very heart of God.

---

6. This is actually a hallmark of the Reformed Tradition—that we discern God's call in community. If a person senses a call to a particular ministry, way of life, or task, that call should be tested and confirmed through conversation and prayer with others. It's a pretty good way to ensure that we don't run off and start dancing around on the town square acting like cats while chanting about the the Flying Spaghetti Monster (no offense meant to his Noodly Appendage!).

We know this is a hard sell in our radically individualistic world. We also know that there are great benefits to be found in engaging with a community seeking the sacred together. Whether we join an established community or gather a new one, the Spirit will be hard at work transforming us into a picture of grace for the world.

When your authors feel discouraged about the state of our community or the difficulty of building real relationships with real (flawed) human beings, we remind ourselves that there is a picture of true community for us to ponder: the Trinity. This is the classic Christian understanding of God as Three-Yet-One. Some have called the Trinity the "pattern of community" and there are prayers that address "God in community, holy and one."

We realize that the doctrine of the Trinity makes very little sense—nearly every sermon ever preached on the topic is mediocre at best—and that this is the kind of leap away from logic that makes organized religion hard to swallow.[7] We also realize that there is something beautiful in the idea that God, all by God's self, is a community, a model for relationship. The Eastern Orthodox talk about the three persons of the Trinity as locked in an eternal dance, weaving and interweaving, always navigating the waters of being together. That resonates with our experience of community all right—probably because we believe that all people are created "in the image of God" and God's image is community!

When we gather into loving community, we are offered a glimpse at the very heart of God. In shared laughter and tears, work and play, we experience love that is more rich and complex than we could imagine on our own. Love, from God. Love which is God.[8] When we join together in faith and hope, we have an opportunity to live into that love.

The fact that we can't fully comprehend the relationship between the Creator, the Son, and the Spirit is a reminder that we can never fully understand another person or the complex web of relationships in which we find ourselves. Our vision is always limited by our own perspective and experience. What we can do is look at the world through the lens of the Trinity, always on the lookout for ways we can engage in relationships with different people, dancing and weaving together something beautiful, where all know themselves as Beloved.

---

7. John Wesley famously said "Bring me a worm that can comprehend a man, and then I will show you a man that can comprehend the triune God!"

8. 1 John 4:16

GOING TO PRACTICE

Invite friends to a story-telling party. Before you gather at your house, a pizza joint, or perhaps a picnic, share a prompt with your friends. Depending on the group and your comfort level it could be something as silly as "share your funniest family holiday story" or as deep as "talk about a time you faced your worst fear." Gather together, eat, and share.

SEE MORE...

David G. Benner, *Sacred Companions* (InterVarsity Press: Downers Grove, IL, 2002).

John O'Donohue, *Eternal Echoes: Celtic Reflections on Our Yearning to Belong* (Harper Perennial: New York, 1999).

SEVEN

〜

BETWEEN THE SHEETS

"Abide with me: fast falls the eventide;
the darkness deepens; Lord, with me abide!"
—HENRY FRANCIS LYTE

We spend one-third of our lives sleeping. This is, of course, very obvious when you think about it—but be honest, when have you ever actually stopped to think about that?

Thirty-three percent of our lives—spent in beds, sleeping bags, couches, chairs, floors, air mattresses—sleeping away time.

Sleep is extremely important—even if our workplaces and schedules usually don't recognize the brilliance of mandated naptime. There's a reason we are supposed to spend eight hours doing it every day. That time we spend sleeping is time our bodies use to repair themselves, fend off disease, grow, and no doubt all kinds of other things that we can read about in science books and journals and blogs. The trouble is, at least in the culture in which we find ourselves, sleep *looks* extremely unproductive, and being unproductive is a cardinal sin. One would think we were created for the purpose of making, doing, fixing, and all kinds of other action-related verbs, because the instant we engage in a passive-sounding verb like resting, sleeping, observing, or even praying, we are looked down upon as lazy, good-for-nothing time wasters.

Lazy?!? We have to work harder than any previous generation to get close to the standard of living our elders are used to, and most of us won't reach it. "Work hard and you'll succeed," shouts the world around us. The problem—aside from the fact that we can only drink so much caffeine to counteract the lack of rest—is this just isn't true for most of us. Instead we will work hard, but know only a shadow of our parents' standard of living and still get called lazy.[1]

We are here to say that it is not lazy or slothful to recognize that we can all use some downtime. In fact, let's just go out on that proverbial limb and say that spending passive time, even wasting time, is good for us and is what God wants us to do sometimes. Contrary to popular belief, "God helps those who help themselves" is *not* in the Bible, but "remember the Sabbath day" is. Sabbath is about stopping and resting, praying and being. It's downtime with the divine. It's not just good for our stress levels; it's good for our spirits.

Hear the word "Sabbath" and think it means one day of the week spent sitting in a straight-backed hard chair from sundown to sundown? We don't blame you. All that cultural memory (for most of us it isn't our own memory, it's one passed down through Little House on the Prairie) of Sundays spent sitting quietly, longing to play outside, or Sundays when stores weren't open and running errands was taboo—those memories are not of true Sabbath keeping, they're of legalistic check-off-the-commandments living.

Nothing about downtime with the divine—or keeping Sabbath as folks used to say—should be legalistic. Yes, it may be a commandment, but remember that the Sabbath was created *for us*, not the other way around. Downtime is something to practice because it reminds us who and Whose we are, and is something to be celebrated as a gift—not something to be turned into yet another thing we "should" *do*. None of us were created to work our lives away, and every day should have some downtime.

Teri's personal go-to downtime activity is, of course, sleeping. She loves to sleep. Eight hours seems like such a puny amount of time to spend doing something so wonderful. What better entry to downtime with the divine, to Sabbath keeping, than this spiritual practice. A spiritual practice that just happens to center around a time when all of us stop and rest and, well, sleep.

Take just a moment and think to yourself:

> When was the last time I tried to pray before bed and actually stayed awake until "amen"?
> When was the last time I felt really focused and listened to what God had to say to me?
> When was the last time I was able to clear my mind and just rest in God's love?

---

1. Even before the economy turned south in 2008, things were looking pretty rough for your average twenty and thirty-somethings. "Young adults are more likely to be unemployed, hold part-time jobs, or work as temps. . .Young adults across the board are earning less today than they would have twenty or thirty years ago . . . Living paycheck to paycheck is the new norm for young adults." Tamara Draut, *Strapped: Why America's 20- and 30-Somethings Can't Get Ahead* (New York: Doubleday, 2006), 10-11.

If any of those questions made your eyes droopy just thinking about them, then between the sheets may be your best place for prayer.

Think about it—the meditation gurus, the yoga masters, the centering prayer experts, even the ministers out there are all telling us to "just let go," "relax," "be in the moment," "empty yourself." Easier said than done, in our experience. Even at the end of yoga class, with the teacher reminding us every minute or so, "no thoughts—just breathing" we still find ourselves making lists, fretting about the time, or wondering if we've forgotten to do anything today.

But when we sleep, all that is exactly what we let go of. Sometimes this can be very hard work. Anxiety, stress, frustration, depression, excitement—all can be hard to release so we can just rest, but anyone who's suffered from insomnia knows that sleep is welcome relief. When we sleep, we clear our conscious mind and let the subconscious take over. When we sleep, we are finally vulnerable and open enough for God to communicate. Sometimes that communication is as simple as waking to find we know the answer to that nagging problem that had been bothering us before we fell asleep. Sometimes it happens through dreams. Sometimes it's just a feeling, a nudge, an inkling. Every time we close our eyes and drift off, we allow ourselves to rest in the love of God, a love deeper and broader than we can possibly imagine. This is exactly what prayer and meditation are all about—resting in the presence of the One who loves more than we can fathom, who is bigger than our imaginations or our rational minds.

We can practically hear you asking the pages of this book *how* to practice sleep as a spiritual discipline. Well, it's pretty simple, really. Lie down. Close your eyes. Give yourself over to God's love. Rest. If it works better for you, start by talking to God and then allow God to talk to you as you sleep. If it helps, lie down and read—read the Bible if you have one handy, read a book of prayers, read theology—even read *this* book if it helps you fall asleep. Instead of *clearing* your mind, *focus* your mind and heart and spirit on God, and just rest. If reading or talking don't work, try imagining—imagine holding yourself in the light. Imagine God holding you in the palm of God's hand. Imagine yourself as part of a story from the Bible. All of these are ways to invite God into your resting, and to give yourself over to prayer and Sabbath-keeping in a way that can be healing for both your body and your soul.

Maybe you're one of those people who wakes up in the middle of the night and has trouble falling asleep again. You're not alone—in fact, it used to be perfectly normal to wake up and do things in the dead of night![2]

---

2. Stephanie Hegarty, "The Myth of the Eight Hour Sleep," BBC (2012): http://www.bbc.co.uk/news/magazine-16964783.

During the Renaissance, people even created special prayer books for that hour or two of wakefulness. Islamic tradition even has a particular prayer (voluntary, in addition to the five required prayers) for night-time, called *Qiyaam al-Layl*. So don't just stare into the darkness or at the creeping clock, but use that time to look for God. Perhaps it's a good time for the practice of *examen* (check out chapter 8 for more on that). Perhaps it would be a time to not just endlessly run through the to-do list but to consciously place each item into the hands of God.

You could also borrow a practice from the monks who wake up in the middle of the night for the Night Watch, and use that wakeful time to "wait for the Lord, more than those who watch for the morning" (Psalm 130). If you want to try out a Night Watch, be sure you go to bed wearing clothes you can go outside in, or keep some outside clothes nearby. If the weather's bad, clear a space near a window. When you awake at that inconvenient time (traditionally it's around 2 or 3am), go outside or to your window. Sit in silence and darkness, allowing your eyes to roam the heavens. Be on the lookout for what God is doing, in the physical world and in your inner world. Enjoy the quiet. Feel the drape of darkness. Allow yourself to sense your part in the cosmos. Listen. If you feel so moved, recite a prayer, song, poem, or scripture that comes to mind. Then head back to bed, ready to allow God to rest in you just as you have rested in God.

Along with watching in the night, you can wait for the dawn, a practice that has a full and rich tradition across the world. One of our favorite observations of this practice occurs at the summit of Haleakala, the east volcano on Maui, where there's a large crater. According to legend, the demigod Maui (from whom the island gets its name) stood in that crater and, as the sun began to rise in the east, he lassoed the sun and would not let go until it agreed to his demand to slow its journey across the sky, lengthening the day for the island's people. Today people gather at the summit in the pre-dawn hour, waiting to catch the first glimpse of the sun rising above the clouds and beginning a new day. As the first ray shines, a National Park ranger breaks out into a chant, welcoming the sun and the day it brings. Not all of us can head over to Maui, but we can try greeting the day. Wake up an hour before the sun is scheduled to rise. Note the changes that are taking place: the colors that begin to dance across the sky, the sounds of the earth coming awake. When you see the first ray of sun, offer up a prayer to God, giving thanks for this new day as well as for the night just past. "O Lord, let my soul rise up to meet you, as the day rises to meet the sun."[3]

---

3. Shane Claiborne, et al., *Common Prayer: a Liturgy for Ordinary Radicals* (Grand Rapids: Zondervan 2010), 49.

THE BEST PART OF WAKING UP?

This may not be true for you, but for many of us (your authors most definitely included) the worst part of sleeping is the waking up. Perhaps what you usually think when you wake up goes something like this: "Oh God, I can't believe it's time to get up. Why is it so hot/so cold/so light/so dark/so not-me-continuing-to-sleep?????" immediately followed by "I wonder when I can get a nap in today?" Or maybe you're one of those folks for whom the first moment of morning is greeted with bounding out of bed. The alarm sounds and you're off! You wake up and hit the ground running.

Whether you groan or greet the day with cheer, consider orienting the new day (or new evening for you nightshift types) around the Center. Neither moaning nor rushing are ideal ways for waking if they don't help you start the day with awareness of the God who grants each day and calls us to live, laugh, and love in it.

> "The older generation thought nothing of getting up at five every morning—and the younger generation doesn't think much of it either."
>
> —JOHN J. WELSH

As you first come to consciousness, rather than jumping straight to the lists of things you need to do or the ways in which you'd prefer to be sleeping, spend a moment centering in the divine. Maybe even offer thanks—thanks for a new beginning, thanks for sleep, thanks for the breath you are taking in. If you aren't in a place where you can offer a genuine "thank you" then perhaps just "good morning" will do. Let your day begin with an awareness that you aren't alone in it.

Maybe even try using your snooze button as a helper to focus on grace—we know that's not what the alarm clock sounds like, but just try it out for a few days. When the alarm goes off, hit that snooze button and spend the next 5-9 minutes (however long until it starts buzzing again!) opening yourself to the movement of the Spirit and wondering what God might have in store for you today. Perhaps set your alarm fifteen minutes early and use the 2-3 snooze opportunities as different types of prayer, first offering thanks, second giving all your worries or fears about the day to God, and third just lying there half awake, listening to the world and the Spirit wake up around you. Or perhaps when the alarm goes off, after you get through the initial shock of waking, call to mind a quote or a song and let it play in your mind for a few minutes. It could be something as simple as "This is the day the Lord has made, I will rejoice and be glad in it" (Psalm 117) or a song that helps you make a connection to something beyond yourself. (Teri's morning brain tends to head for the Indigo Girls while Amy's enjoys some rockin' 70s power ballads—any song will do.) It's okay to drift in and out—that liminal space in our consciousness is perfect for God to move in. Before you know it, you'll have simultaneously accidentally and intentionally chatted with God for several minutes. What better way to wake up than easing into the day via a holy moment?

If you remember dreams, it might be helpful to keep a dream journal. You'll need to do this immediately when you wake up. The instructions are simple: just write. Write everything you remember. Images, feelings, people, places. Then ask yourself whether your dream reminds you of any other parts of God's great story (whether in the Bible, throughout history, or in your own life). What is God trying to communicate? Or what is your subconscious telling you? Write these things down, and then come back to the journal later (at the end of the day, at the end of the week—whenever works for you) and see if there are new messages emerging, new images presenting themselves, new ideas you're open to considering. Remember, when you're asleep is often when you're most open to God speaking— your mental, rational, and emotional defenses are down. There's a reason dreams play a big part in the Bible, from Joseph to Samuel to the prophets to Peter![4]

It's true that sometimes dreams are just weird. Don't get wrapped up in thinking every single dream has a deep spiritual meaning—occasionally the pink koala driving the yellow convertible that magically becomes a golden retriever to paddle across the river is just your subconscious having a good time with you, or a sign that it's time to step away from the Netflix. However, we often rationalize our way out of communiqués from God during waking hours in a way that we can't do when we're asleep. We turn problems over and over in our minds, worrying away at them like knots that get tighter and tighter. The Spirit can sometimes speak through our sleeping subconscious, unraveling the knot just enough that a solution becomes clear or a way forward presents itself. The same can be true of narrative dreams—these stories created while we sleep can carry the symbols that connect us to what God is doing through us, or to the calling God has for us, if only we will notice them.

---

4. Unfamiliar with these stories? Here's a brief summary: Joseph took the circuitous route to becoming Pharaoh's right hand man, thanks to his dreams (see Genesis 37-50); Samuel heard the voice of God while snoozing (see 1 Samuel 3); Peter had this wacky dream involving animals descending from the sky on a sheet—all to teach him about being more open-minded and inclusive (see Acts 10).

PIOUS PLEASURE

While you're between the sheets, if you're involved in a loving, committed, life-affirming relationship, there's nothing wrong with a little fun (even a little…ahem…productivity) going on too! Sexual intimacy is part of what God desires for us, when it's healthy and loving and affirming. It also certainly can be an important part of keeping the Sabbath—it is something that can be life-renewing, can help us experience ourselves and be loved, and can even be restful and rejuvenating at the same time.

Sexual intimacy as Sabbath may be a challenging concept for some of us. Too many religious communities have separated the sensual from the sacred. This separation goes against the tradition of God as a lover and physical love as a holy gift from God, which is as old as any of our sacred texts. Religious mystics, including the Islamic saint Rabia (717-801), write about God in ways that'd make even Sex and the City characters blush. And if you want to talk about hot, check out one of the best erotic love poems of all time: Song of Songs. "How much better is your love than wine. . .Your lips distill nectar, my bride; honey and milk are under your tongue. . .

> "One day He did not leave after kissing me."
>
> —RABIA OF BASRA[5]

Let my beloved come to his garden, and eat its choicest fruits. . . Eat, friends, drink and be drunk with lovemaking" (Song 4:10–11, 16 and 5:1).[6] Don't let any Puritanical notions squash your spiritual self. Embrace your sexuality as part of your spirituality while you're embracing your loved one.

Like many spiritual practices, sexual intimacy can become Sabbath when our hearts are set not just on what we are doing but what God may be doing in the moment too. Pay attention with all your senses. As you appreciate the physical and emotional aspects of intimacy, be open to the spiritual. We are created beings full of sensory possibilities, and by being present to the joy and sensations of an intimate moment, we can experience ourselves so fully alive that something we can't intellectually comprehend may happen. Without even trying, through sexual intimacy you may have a spiritual experience—or at least something you may interpret as such later. In the flow of pleasure and love, know that all the joy you are

---

5. Daniel Ladinsky, trans., *Love Poems from God: Twelve Sacred Voices from the East and West* (New York: Penguin Group, 2002), 3.

6. Author's translation. Note: this book is also called Song of Solomon so don't be confused if you can't find Song of Songs in a Bible.

experiencing is a gift from God. Revel not just in the sensation of being touched but the sensation of touching, and give yourself over to the experience in all its glory—the tastes, the smells, the pheromones! Note the sounds of your partner's breathing, your breathing. Truly feel that connection, that melding into one, and know that this is a holy moment.

Our senses are part of God's creation and what excites them leads us to form a bond that is unlike any other—that feeling of unity and oneness with another human being. What a gift for those of us seeking healthy, loving community! And remember: if it's not affirming and loving (not just in the emotional sense of the word but in the action sense—love as self-giving and all-encompassing), it's not Sabbath, and it's also probably not worth it.

If you are not in a loving, life-affirming relationship, or if your relationship isn't at that point just yet, don't think that your sexual side is off-limits to your spiritual life. Appreciating the gift of sexuality does not require two to tango. Whether with a loving partner or with self-love, the ways in which our complex bodies can create pleasurable feelings should be appreciated—no, not just appreciated, be *cause* for us to shout out praises of thanksgiving. Don't be ashamed to explore the body God gave you, to know yourself in all your physical, sensual glory. Use all your senses to delight in this gift, and however you find yourself saying "O God, O God," give yourself permission for that to be a genuine prayer.

LOUNGING FOR THE LORD

If you do find yourself with a whole day of rest to observe and celebrate the gift of downtime, may we recommend Teri's favorite pastime: a pajama day. It's just what it sounds like—spend the whole day in your pajamas (even if it is Tuesday)! Read, eat, nap whenever your eyes get heavy, sit by the window and just stare, watch movies, catch a basketball tournament on ESPN, clean if you must, surf the Internet, play Facebook games, play with your pets, talk on the phone—anything you want, whenever it strikes your fancy. Just stay in your PJs all day. You'll be surprised how luxurious it feels, how restful it seems—even to do housework in pajamas feels somehow more relaxed. There's something about an entire day spent wearing the clothes we wear for sleeping that feels like downtime, like a gift to be used however we please, like unproductive time during which others can't make demands on us in the same way they can when we're wearing work clothes and we're on the clock. It opens the mind, the heart, and the spirit to the movement of God's breath, to hear the still small voice. Many a brilliant idea and meaningful prayer have come during naps on pajama days. Again, we find a thin place (where the boundary between our life experience and the kingdom of God is "thin") in that liminal space between asleep and awake, and it's as holy as any pilgrimage site—and a pajama day full of short naps allows plenty of holy places to emerge. Try it out! Don't have a whole day? Try just changing into your PJs when you're home for only an hour or two. It really does set apart that restful time.

Whether you spend a whole day, a few hours, or just a good night's sleep between the sheets, you can't help but keep it holy if you remember it is God's good gift. Resting in God is certainly more than simply physical rest, but this is a wonderful place to start. Remember the first creation story found in Genesis: after creating all that is seen and unseen, what did God do? God had a pajama day. If it's good enough for the Creator, it's good enough for the creation. Rest, relax, and just be.

GOING TO PRACTICE
Borrow an idea from the authors of *Way To Live*[7] and take a 15-minute N.A.P—a Non-Active-Period. Just spend 15 minutes *today* not doing anything productive—whether that's a walk outside, some time just staring into space, or a nap. A snippet of Sabbath!

SEE MORE...
Wayne Mueller, *Sabbath: Finding Rest, Renewal, and Delight in Our Busy Lives* (New York: Bantam Books, 1999).

---

7. Dorothy C. Bass and Don C. Richter, eds., *Way to Live* (Nashville: Upper Room Books, 2002), 139-153.

EIGHT

BRINGING IT FORWARD

"It's all been done before!"
—BARENAKED LADIES[1]

"When I was your age…"
"If you want my advice…"
"You know, if it were me…"
Depending on the situation and who's talking, that's either the prelude to some good advice or the beginning of patronizing, paternalistic lecture.

Our parents' generation—or for some of us even our grandparents'—coined the phrase "don't trust anyone over thirty." And yet, as they've gotten older, that attitude has changed to something more like "don't trust anyone *under* thirty." The generation that fought the Man and the system and threw over the way things had always been done now looks at the next generation and wants respect, and an attentive audience.

Not that our generation is innocent of all such comments. Both of your authors have experienced that moment of looking at newbies in our field and thinking "oh, aren't they cute" even as we turned and offered unwanted advice. Pot kettle much?

The unwanted, patronizing words of "wisdom" are rarely, if ever, helpful. But there is some good within that desire to share what we've learned. The experience and wisdom of generations past, while not always welcome, can be genuinely beneficial. We don't have to reinvent the wheel every time. Sure, we can make it sturdier or safer, but we don't have to start

---

1. Barenaked Ladies, *It's All Been Done,* Reprise, 1999, CD.

from scratch. Of course, you don't want to bring every ancient practice forward (let's leave mole shirts and self-flagellation behind, thank you). But there are some wonderful traditions that hold up over time. Sometimes the *tried and true* is called such for a good reason, not because we're too lazy or comfortable to think up something new.

In this chapter, we explore practices rooted in ancient tradition and offer the occasional contemporary twist. When we engage in these practices, not only are we engaging in something "time tested," but we are entering into that awesome spectrum of seekers. Folks from across the ages have sought God using these practices. And now it's our turn to take part in these classic means of coming to know the divine and coming to be at peace within ourselves.

CENTERING PRAYER

"I can't pray."

We hear this a whole heck of a lot. It's usually not true. Yes, there are times when we really can't pray—we don't have the heart for it and all we can say is, "I wish I wanted to pray." But usually when people say they can't pray, they don't mean the will to pray has left the building. Rather, people both in our churches and our communities often feel like they don't know *how* to pray, or they wouldn't be "good" at it, or they'll say or do the wrong thing and mess up the whole cosmic order. As if you spoke a prayer and it didn't sound like something Maya Angelou would say, then it must be crap.

Not true. The only thing that stinks around here is the idea that prayer is only for certain people who know just the right words or have the purest hearts.

Prayer is really not that complicated. In fact, it's as simple as breathing. Don't know where to start when it comes to prayer? Try this. Breathe in deep, let the breath out slowly. Ta-Da! You just prayed. At the very least you started to center your being, which is the beginning of prayer. Prayer at its core orients us toward the Holy One. Taking a moment to observe a deep breath brings us back to the one who breathed life into us. If you have more than a moment, spend some time taking deep, intentional breaths. Get comfortable. Go ahead and tell God you'd like a little holy moment as you breathe. Let those breaths chase away stress or worry, busyness or boredom. Let them welcome in a sense of the divine.

If you don't have more than a moment, you can still let the breath of God be your breath. After all, it's not like you can just stop breathing because you're too busy. An awareness of the gift of breathing can be enough—this is about looking in a new way at something you already do. So remember, if you can breathe, you can pray!

This simple idea of using your breath as a way to center yourself is ancient. So ancient we don't know who first came up with idea. However, we do know who popularized the variation on this theme: centering prayer. Back in the 1970s a group of Trappist[2] monks offered up their own contribution to bringing the old ways forward. Basing their practice on a fourteenth century anonymous classic called *The Cloud of Unknowing*, these religious men developed, and soon spread, this ancient-modern prayer.

Centering prayer is as easy as adding a word to your breath prayer. Specifically, a word that is sacred to you. Perhaps this word is what you're seeking (peace, joy, hope), or perhaps it invokes a sense of the divine (spirit, water, light). Your word can change from prayer to prayer, or if you find one that really centers you, feel free to keep with it. Whatever your word may be, as you breathe in and breathe out, let yourself sink into the space your breath and word create, the images and feelings that bubble up. When your mind begins to wander (and it will), bring yourself back to your word.

If you've tried simple breathing with a word and would like to do something a little different, try using a short phrase. Maybe something from scripture like "Be still and know that I am God" or "Good news of great joy for all people."[3] Or maybe something from other wise voices like "all shall be well" or "*Baruch ata Adonai*" (blessed are you, O Lord).[4] Don't pick anything too long—you don't want to be breathing in and out and discover yourself rushing through the phrase as fast as you can in your mind to squeeze the whole dang thing in. You might start out thinking the whole phrase with each breath or half of the phrase as you breathe in, the second half as you breathe out. Try slowing it down: focus on one word of your phrase per breath. Some people even add a pause between the inhale and the exhale (briefly holding breath in, or feeling the emptiness before inhaling again) to help them center.

As you breathe, think about your word or phrase, and let this be an agenda-free time. Don't enter into centering prayer and think "today, I'm going to get all the answers I've ever wanted" or even "I am going to have an awesome moment with the divine." Just breathe and be. Enter into that great cloud of unknowing where things can happen—but where they

---

2. The Trappists are a religious order which follows the Rule of St. Benedict and are rightfully known for their great beer.
3. Psalm 46:10; Luke 2:10.
4. From a prayer by Julian of Norwich and from traditional Jewish prayers, respectively.

don't always. Don't feel bad if you try this prayer style and rarely (if ever) have that transcendent moment. This is a prayer that probably needs to be repeated a lot before you can really get into it. Thank goodness you can do it almost anywhere. On the subway, at the Laundromat, at a really boring meeting—anywhere! And don't feel you need to do this for hours on end. Up to twenty minutes is likely more than enough. While the apostle Paul said we should "pray without ceasing" (1 Thess. 5:17), he never said we had to pray the same way that whole time. As Thomas Keating says, "your prayer should normally finish before you develop a sore back!"[5]

GUIDED MEDITATION

Like many of our ancient practices, we don't know who first came up with the idea of meditation. References first appear in written form as far back as 1500 B.C.E and meditation itself pops up in various forms in many—if not most—of the world's religions. We also don't know who first thought of helping each other out when trying to meditate. Maybe it's just an innate part of the human experience: we all need a little help from our friends.

If you have trouble staying focused by yourself and need peer pressure—uh, *support*—to keep your focus, or perhaps you'd like to grow deeper into your already rich prayer life, then consider guided meditation. What is guided meditation? Well, exactly what it sounds like: meditation that's guided! Rather than trying to focus on your breath or a word by yourself, someone provides imagery or words to focus you. This "someone" can be live and in the flesh, or via a podcast or phone app or a website or anywhere else you might find aid.[6]

Anywhere? Yes, anywhere. Even while watching TV. *The Daily Show* has those moments of Zen, which are usually hilarious but rarely lead to introspection like a good Zen meditation might. However, as we write this book, a cruise line is putting out commercials consisting of peaceful footage of a sunset over the ocean or ice falling off a glacier into the sea. These 20 seconds or so aren't just peace; they end with a title screen in which the company takes credit for that moment of relaxation. But in those 20 seconds prior to the company logo, maybe you can get a little help in the meditation department.

If you're interested in trying guided meditation (without having to wait for a commercial), here is a brief meditation you can try with some friends.

---

5. Thomas Keating, *Open Mind, Open Heart* (New York: Continuum, 2000), 59.
6. A couple of good podcasts and phone apps can be found (as of this book's publication) at meditationoasis.com.

Create sacred space in time and place using chimes, a bell, a singing bowl, or some other peaceful sound to help focus and mark this time apart.

Invite participants to breathe in. Then breathe out. Breathe in. Breathe out. Breathe in the day's joy. Breathe out the day's stress. Breathe in. Breathe out. Breathe in God's mercies. Breathe out God's mercies to others.

If you'd like to try meditation with some imagery, here's one to try:

Sit up, straight yet comfortable, and relax your shoulders. Take a deep breath in, and let it out slowly. Breathe in God's spirit of grace, and breathe that spirit out to others.
Listen.
…

Jesus is teaching, beside the lake.
What do you see?
What do you smell?
What can you feel on your skin?
What do you hear?
…

Listen.
…

A farmer went out to plant his field,
and he scattered seeds far and wide.

Feel the ground, smell the soil, hear the other plants rustling.
Feel the warm air, the light breeze.
Small seeds, each containing a germ of life…

Listen.
…

The path is hard ruts, from people and animals walking.
There's hardly room to breath, everything is so tightly packed.

The rocks too are hard. They clutter the ground
and it's hard to move around them.

The weedy thorns have thick roots, intertwined through the dirt,
    cares and distractions gobbling up precious nutrients.

Prepared soil…a perfect mix of dirt and water and oxygen and
    nutrients.
Is there a resting place, a nurturing place, a place that calls out
    what is inside?
Slowly and yet at exactly the right time, life takes shape, springs
    forth, pushes out…
the harvest is beyond imagining.

Which soil do you find yourself in?
Are you resting on hard packed road, traveling in a bird, being
    trampled?
Are you bursting up through the rocks, wondering where the
    food and water are, trying to bring something out of nothing?
Are you fighting your way through the weeds while your roots
    choke beneath the surface?
Are you resting in the dark soil, growing slowly yet perfectly, nur-
    tured and nourished, connected to your source, filled to an
    overflowing harvest?

Listen.
…

Where are you planted?
…

Listen.
God says,
"as the rain and the snow come down from heaven
and do not return until they accomplish that which I purpose,
so will my word be.
It shall not return to me empty."

That which God purposes
will not return empty.

The germ inside the seed will spring up, bringing life.
The soil may be prepared, or it may not,
but the kingdom will rise up in us.

God calls it forth, no matter the circumstances in which you find
yourself.

Are you connected to the Source? Can you connect now?

Are you nourished and nurtured? Jesus said, "ask and you will receive"—ask now for what you need to grow in God's harvest.

Are you rising up to be who God calls you to be?
Listen…

A sower went out to sow.
The seed went to every place, every time, every kind of life,
every kind of experience.
That which God purposes will not return empty.

Let anyone with ears listen.

IGNATIAN EXAMEN

If you've ever been a part of a church youth group, you may have experienced a form of Saint Ignatius' famous spiritual practice, where you share
the awesome and annoying parts of your day. Highs and Lows. Yeas and
Nays. Roses and Thorns. Happies and Crappies (that last one is Amy's
favorite version). It's a good way to decompress and process a day, which is
probably why so many youth groups use that model when on mission trips
or at church camps. Of course, spending time thinking about the day, the
good and not so good, is not exclusive to sitting around the campfire singing "Sanctuary." While he didn't start the concept of a daily review either,
Ignatius of Loyola, founder of the Society of Jesus (a.k.a. the Jesuits), did
write about and encourage reflection in such a meaningful way that he gets
a lot of credit for making the practice popular.

Drawing from Ignatius' book on spiritual practices (appropriately
titled *Exercitia Spiritualia*—"spiritual exercises" in Latin), try this classic
examen, also called "examination of consciousness."

When you wake up, set a goal for your day—to avoid a particular failing or feeling, or perhaps to do more good that day. At mid-day, check in
with yourself. How are you doing on your goal so far? Ask for strength
and grace to keep your resolve. At the end of the day, as you lay down to
rest, check in again. How did you do? How do you feel about your goal?

For where you met your desire, rejoice. For where you fell short, forgive yourself. Go to bed knowing you've spent a day seeking your best self and be at peace.

A common variation on the classic has the *examen* only at the end of the day. Interested? Here's how to begin:

- ❧ Seek the presence of the divine. A few deep breaths or perhaps the recitation of holy words can root you in sacred soil.
- ❧ Give thanks to God for some big picture stuff (not necessarily a great moment in your day—that'll come later—but for the day itself). With a heart toward thanksgiving, ask God to help you to see yourself as loved. Knowing you are loved—feeling that love—will set the rest of the examen in the best light.
- ❧ Think about your day. Where did you feel God today? Was there a moment where you felt you were in the presence of the Holy? Where you caught a glimpse of the sacred? Reflect on that moment. If you can recall details of that moment, do.
- ❧ Ask yourself where you felt God's presence the least. Was it a moment of despair? A moment of disappointment in yourself? Recall that moment, but do not dwell. Take a breath and release that memory.
- ❧ Ask God to help you savor the joys of the day, learn from the disappointments, and find rest in a day come to its end.

Other *examen* reflections you might choose to use are:

- ❧ For what am I grateful/least grateful?
- ❧ What about today would I like to live again/avoid in the future?
- ❧ Where did I feel in sync/out of step with God?

When you have finished reviewing your day, make sure you end on a positive note. That may mean going back to the place of thanksgiving or thinking about a joy of the day or spending more time in the loving presence of God. The *examen* is not about beating yourself up. It's about taking in the day and reflecting on it within the loving presence of the Holy One. Reflect on your day and rest in God's love.

PRAYER BEADS

If your main reference for this particular prayer accessory is the celebrity fashion trend made most famous by Madonna, don't worry: we're not trying to reclaim that look. Leave the rosary-and-corset combos to the celebutantes. Let us instead try to incorporate this ancient method of prayer into our lives, not our outfits—though you might want to consider keeping a strand of beads in your coat pocket and using them to pray as you walk to work, ride the bus, or stand in the checkout line. Teri can tell you from personal experience that feeling in your pocket the string of beads representing "love, joy, peace, patience, kindness, generosity, faithfulness, gentleness, and self control"[7] will drastically change the way you respond to the person in front of you in the express line, especially if they have more than 20 items.

Prayer beads are a fabulous means to keep focused on your conversation with God—whether you're in the talking or listening mode. Whether you're repeating a Hail Mary or a verse of scripture, the repetition of holy words can help chase out the voices of busyness, stress, or uncertainty. The tactile element that comes with touching the beads can make concrete the prayers of your heart. Closing your eyes, holding the bead between your thumb and index finger, opening yourself to the mystery of God: many different traditions include such a practice. Roman Catholics have the rosary where Hail Marys, Lord's Prayers, and Glory Be to the Fathers are said; the Islamic tradition includes the use of a *misbaha* to recite prayers; practitioners of Hinduism and Buddhism use the *Japa Mala* to keep track of the recitation of chants or names of deities; the Eastern Orthodox traditions often use knots in a rope rather than beads to recite the "Jesus Prayer."[8] These traditions suggest that the best way to use prayer beads is to pick a few phrases, words, or prayers to meditate on, and repeat those holy words as you go along your prayer strand.

Here are a couple of different meditations we've used and found helpful.

Using a standard Dominican rosary:[9]

- ❦ Begin your prayer time offering up to the divine what you are seeking (energy, peace, hope, rest, etc.).
- ❦ Offer up a prayer from tradition—perhaps the Lord's Prayer, perhaps St. Francis of Assisi's prayer—at the single (often larger) bead.
- ❦ For the groupings of ten beads, offer up the first line of the prayer you have chosen or perhaps another complementary holy phrase. Take a deep breath at each bead.

---

7. The "fruits of the spirit" are described in Galatians 5:22-23.
8. Lord Jesus Christ, Son of God, have mercy on me, a sinner.
9. There are several varieties of rosaries but the ones you are probably most familiar with (and/or likely to get a hold of) include a circle made of five sets of ten beads with a single bead separating each set. These ten bead sets are called decades. Hanging off the circle of beads is a pendant comprised of one large bead, three small beads, another large bead, and a crucifix.

❧ Continue this pattern until you reach the end/beginning of the circle.

❧ Follow down along the pendant and offer the ancient prayer at the larger beads. At the smaller beads, offer up again what you are seeking.

❧ Come to the crucifix, pause. Take three deep intentional breaths, and then conclude with an "Amen."

Using a *Japa Mala*:[10]

❧ Choose three names for God which have significant meaning for you (e.g., HaShem, Ancient of Days, Most Merciful, Timeless One). One bead, one name, one breath. Next bead, another name, another breath. Third bead, third name, deep breath.

❧ Continue along the strand. When you complete the circle, conclude with a short prayer.

Since you can purchase many of the traditional prayer beads through that ginormous marketplace, Amazon, or through local religious centers or bookstores, you don't need to be crafty to own some prayer beads, though making your own can be meaningful too.

PRAYER FLAGS

If you are into arts 'n' crafts, let's talk about prayer flags. If you've ever been hiking in the Himalayas, you've probably run into these fabric prayers. Never been hiking in Nepal? Okay, well, if you've seen pictures of that region, or been into an alternative bookstore or known practicing Buddhists, we'd bet you've seen those colorful rectangles blowing in the breeze. The pieces of fabric are covered in symbols, mantras, and words that speak of goodness, hope, peace, joy, good fortune. Placed on a rope or strong cord, the decorated rectangles not only provide a bit of color to the countryside but blessing as well. As the wind blows through the flags, the prayers are carried wherever that wind may blow—upon one's town or far away, to neighbors or strangers—those that are touched by the wind are touched by the prayers. How great is that? Prayers for you and from you but not just about you!

---

10. If you use a Japa Mala, you may discover a symbol that seems out of place for an item meant for prayer—the swastika. While best known in the Western world as a symbol associated with Nazism, it is much more ancient (and agreeable) than that. In Eastern traditions, it is a sacred symbol with variations of meaning (eternity, wellness, good fortune).

Prayer flags can be purchased at your local sacred bookstore or online. Find yourself running away in terror from anything crafty? Go ahead and buy some pre-made ones. Just like you can use another person's prayers and find meaning, you can certainly use premade prayer flags. But if you've got a little crafty gumption or even skill, consider making your own. You can create your own prayer flags or join in with friends or family to make community prayer flags. The creation of the flags themselves are a time of reflection and connection with God.

DIY PRAYER FLAGS

TO START YOUR PRAYER FLAGS, think about what it is you want to pray for. What prayers do you want to be lifted up into the wind? What prayers does your community need, your family, you? Come up with at least five different prayers (e.g., faith, unity, peace, joy, wholeness, forgiveness, contentment, healing, goodness, love, wisdom, etc.).

GO TO YOUR LOCAL FABRIC STORE.[11] Pick out colorful fabrics (you'll want at least a couple colors, three to four being traditional). You'll also want to pick up some plain white fabric. How much fabric do you need? That's going to depend on how many flags you want and how big you want them to be. Go ahead and pick up some thread, fabric glue, and durable rope. (It doesn't actually have to be rope, just something you can string from trees or posts or wherever you're planning on hanging your flags. Remember, think durable and strong).

ONCE YOU'RE HOME, cut your colorful fabric into rectangles. Make sure you cut them large enough so that when you place the white fabric on top of your colorful fabric, there will be enough for a border *and* enough to wrap one edge around your rope. Cut the white fabric rectangles. Now, go to town! Get out some (not washable) markers and decorate the white fabric pieces. For each flag, include a written prayer (a word or perhaps a phrase) and some meaningful symbols that correlate with your written prayer. Seeking peace? Include a peace sign or an olive branch or a white poppy. Praying for unity? Draw a rainbow or a circle or clasped hands.

---

11. Don't have easy access to fabric? You can use paper instead—it just won't be as durable/weather-resistant.

WHEN YOU'RE THINKING about the symbols you're going to draw, you can use traditional symbols. Google your word and see what images pop up. You can also use something which has meaning for you. If, for example, when you think of love you think of the chocolate chip cookies your grandmother always made for you, draw chocolate chip cookies. If you hear the word wisdom and see the Enterprise figurine that always sat on your favorite teacher's desk, put that on your flag.

ONCE YOU'VE DECORATED the white parts of your flags, take your colored rectangles, your fabric glue, your thread, and your rope and have yourself a construction party. Glue the white fabric to the larger colorful pieces. Once you've done that, get your completed flags, the thread, and rope (and a needle!). Wrap the longer colorful border around your rope and sew it tightly to the flag. Not really confident with a needle? You can try the fabric glue or do what people have been doing since the beginning of time (… okay, at least since 1942): use duct tape. Leave room between each flag as you go. Flags attached? Congrats! You've just made your own prayer flags. Go find somewhere to hang them!

MOOD LIGHTING

In our hyper-connected culture, it's common for people to spend more time online than in the same physical space with people. In our workaholic world we often forget that we are more than just a job we can do, more than the activities on our résumés. Sometimes we just need a little downtime, a little space for ourselves, a few minutes or an evening or a weekend without interruptions from email, Facebook, "urgent" text messages. If you ever feel that way, you might consider reaching back into the Jewish tradition for some help marking off that time away from the daily grind. Since the middle ages our observant Jewish friends have marked the Sabbath, the day of rest, each Friday evening by lighting candles a few minutes before sunset. These candles will remain lit as a reminder of what time it is—off-the-grid, holy time—all the way until sunset on Saturday night. Those 24 hours are sacred space designed to remind us that the world will go on even if we don't work as though we hold it up by ourselves. A few hours (or even a few days) off will not mean the end of life as we know it. Well, we take that back. It might mean the end of life as we know it because once we've had a taste of rest, we won't want to go back to the endless cycle of expectations to work harder! Faster! Better! Stronger!

Our Jewish friends mark that time with candles because, in more Orthodox teaching, any work is forbidden on the Sabbath, and that includes using electricity, cooking, driving, or doing things that cause others to work (such as eating out). All the preparation for the Sabbath is done in advance, and once the candles are lit, everyone sits and rests together. Most of us are not going to be that strict, but the idea of using candles to mark downtime is a good one. Perhaps you'll light the candles some Sunday afternoon, and say a few words committing your last non-work weekend hours to resting and refreshing. Maybe you'll light the candles as a symbol of living by a light other than the computer screen. Maybe you'll make one hour a week an Earth Hour, when you keep the lights off and read or eat or talk by candlelight, using no electricity. However you do it, lighting Shabbat candles and taking some time out of the daily grind can be an important ritual: resting and reminding yourself that you're part of something bigger.

CONFESSION

". . . what happens when people stop being polite and start getting real."

If you had access to MTV as a kid, you might have grown up hearing that phrase over and over again as you watched fights, hook-ups, and melodrama to the max. *The Real World* put reality television on the map and introduced audiences all over to the reimagined concept of the confessional. Wanted to complain about a roommate? Confessional. Wanted to giggle about what you and another roommate did in the shower? Confessional. Wanted to "get real" by entering a small, secluded room and baring your inner thoughts and feelings to a camera and eventually the world? Confessional.

> Things aren't always right with us and we'd like to do something about it.

It may be hyper-dramatized and sexualized, but the Real World confessional did capture part of the true spirit of confession: it's not something to do lightly. On the show, you couldn't go into the confessional and just say whatever you wanted and expect no consequences.[12] Sure, your roommates don't see/hear it now, but once your season hits the airwaves, they and your mother and your neighbor and that guy at grocery store will all know. What you say has weight to it, consequences. It matters.

---

12. Well, if you were in the right state of mind and not under the influence of alcohol, drugs, or attention/thrill seeking, you'd know this!

Confession itself is an ancient practice that goes back further than video cameras or confessional booths (both the MTV and more traditional religious kinds). Whether through prayers or sacrifices or ritual cleansings, people of the world's religions have been confessing for eons. While the theologies and particulars may vary, in this ancient practice people admit to themselves and to a higher power that they have done wrong, and they seek change.

Depending on your church context (if any) you may have different reactions to the concept of confession. It can seem dogmatic or unnecessary or just plain strange. But it can also feel freeing. Unlike modernists who think human progress always leads toward some almighty good, we who live in the aftermath of the A-bomb, who see young black men being killed simply because they're walking in the wrong neighborhood while an African-American president sits in the Oval Office, who observe all this wonderful science and healing power being used to make pharmaceutical corporations big bucks—we know that our human progress does not always lead to good. We have things as a group, and as individuals, that we need to 'fess up to and strive to turn away from. And this is what confession is really about. Not dogma or empty ritual but acknowledging that things aren't always right with us and we'd like to do something about it.

When we confess, what we say matters. Why? We're not just admitting wrong, but asking for help to do the right thing on the next go-round. There are things we want to change, things we want to do better, things we want to resist, and the act of confession is one beautiful, ancient way we commit ourselves to turning toward the good we long to do and be.

If you'd like to start simple, try a modification of the Jesus Prayer: *Lord, have mercy upon me, a sinner.*

Those seven words are a great place to start. In them you can acknowledge that you are flawed, that you do indeed sin and that you need help.[13] What's that saying—the first step to recovery is admitting you have a problem? With a prayer this simple, you've begun that journey.

If you'd like to expand on that simple prayer, here are a couple of prayer ideas:

   ✤ Enter into your time of prayer with a simple verbal offering: *Holy One, forgive me the things I have done which I should not have done, and the things I have failed to do which I should have done.* Now

---

13. What is sin? That word gets thrown around a lot, but what exactly does it mean? What exactly are we confessing? There are a lot of definitions for sin but perhaps the simplest is this: that which goes against the person/people God wants us to be. Yup, sin can certainly be something that's individual, but it can also be something that's communal.

think about these "things"—name them, in voice or in heart. Don't consider this a laundry list of your failings but a chance to be completely open and honest before the Source of All Good. When you've finished reflecting on your confession, ask for strength to do better the next day.

 Reflect on one failing or fault you'd particularly like to address. Lift up your desire to change with a simple prayer. For example: *Set me free from a past that I cannot change; open to me a future in which I can be changed; and grant me grace to grow more and more in your likeness and image.*[14] Now listen. Be open to what God may have to say or how the divine may move through you and in you.

Want to put your confession out there in a more concrete way? Consider joining the ranks of thousands before you who confessed their sins and/or secrets on-line. No, we're not talking about misguided status updates on Facebook. Try instead PostSecret. If you're not familiar with the website or books, PostSecret is an online community where people mail in home-made postcards with their secrets written on them.[15] Get a blank postcard (or some cardstock cut to postcard size). Get magazines or markers or paints or whatever medium you want. Create images of what it is you wish to confess—literal or abstract. Put into words the confession of your heart. If you and art are like oil and water, just use words to let go and put out into the world something that's been lurking deep inside. What next? You can mail it to PostSecret, of course, but you can also burn it in that age-old way or, if you like a contemporary twist, shred it. You've confessed: you've put what you want to change out there in some tangible way.

If you'd really like to explore the power of confession, consider confessing to someone else. Putting your sin out there, not just between you and God, but between you and another human being and God, takes a lot of guts. By sharing with another person your prayers of confession and desire to grow, you can find you have a friend along the journey. Whether you speak to a counselor or a trusted friend, knowing that someone is aware of your desire for change can help keep you on your path.

The earth mounds of the American Indians, the watchtowers of the Great Wall of China, the ruins of a Scottish castle, the majesty of a medieval

---

14. Adapted from a prayer of confession from *Book of Common Worship* on page 79.
15. Check out the site at www.postsecret.com.

cathedral: standing in or on these ancient monuments to human achievement and imagination infuses you with a sense of history. You know that people of a different age and culture were once exactly where you are, building, creating, working, dreaming, living. How can you not but marvel in knowing you're walking where your ancestors in the human race once walked?

We hope these ancient spiritual practices may provide a similar sense of awe and connectedness. In the Christian tradition we speak about the cloud of witnesses—those who have come before in the faith. People who have lived faith-infused lives, who have not always believed without doubt but who have lived without fear. People who have found the courage and the desire to engage God in their daily lives through some of the practices we've just looked at. In knowing that someone else has been where you are, walked a similar path, known what you've known and even felt what you've felt, may you be strengthened in your journey. We hope that as you take up a practice that women and men across the ages have engaged in their own spiritual journeys, you may feel connected to seekers across time and place. May that connection enrich your own experience of these practices.

GOING TO PRACTICE

Dividing the day into periods which each begin with prayer is a common practice in many faith traditions. For a day or even a week, practice praying the Daily Office or Liturgy of the Hours. There's morning prayer, daytime prayer, evening prayer, and nighttime prayer. Pick a time that works for you for each (or just one or two) hour of prayer. If you were hanging out in a monastery, there'd likely be a bell to call you to prayer. Assuming you're not hanging out by old bell towers, set your cellphone alarm instead. You can use prayer books (like the one mentioned below), an app or podcast (just search for *divine office*), or develop your own prayer practice. Perhaps read a psalm and offer a short prayer at each prescribed prayer time.

SEE MORE...

Celtic Daily Prayer, Northumbria Community (HarperCollins: New York, 2002).

Phyllis Tickle, *The Divine Hours* (New York: Oxford University Press, 2007).

NINE

THIS *IS* REAL LIFE

"Our goal is to connect everyone in the world..."
—FROM THE PINTEREST MISSION STATEMENT

Blogs. Facebook. Vine. Twitter. LinkedIn. YouTube. Pinterest. Google+. Snapchat. Foursquare. Words With Friends. Goodreads. Tumblr. Instagram. Plus, of course, email and text messaging.

The list goes on and on—every day there are new apps and networks that allow us to share our lives, connect with friends and strangers, and converse with the world. We are more connected now than ever before. Or are we?

Research is conflicted on this—some say we are more connected, with more diversity in our networks than ever.[1] Some say we are more isolated than ever, that we spend more time alone and in front of screens instead of with people, now averaging around 8-9 hours a day of screen time (including work).[2] Others wonder about the impact of social media on our actual social connection, insisting that when our connections are primarily online, that allows us to sculpt and edit our identity and to plan our interactions in ways that we can't do if we're talking with people in real life.[3]

The thing is, in an age when many of our relationships develop first (or even only) online, the line between what's "real" and "virtual" is pretty

1. Keith Hampton, Lauren Sessions Goulet, Eun Ja Her, Lee Rainie, "Social Isolation and New Technology," *Pew Internet and American Life Project*, November 4, 2009, http://pewinternet.org/Reports/2009/18--Social-Isolation-and-New-Technology/Executive-Summary/Findings.aspx.
2. Brian Stelter, "8 Hours a Day Spent on Screens, Study Finds," *New York Times* March 26, 2009, http://www.nytimes.com/2009/03/27/business/media/27adco.html.
3. Sherry Turkle, "Alone Together," *TED talk February 2012*, http://www.ted.com/talks/sherry_turkle_alone_together.html.

blurry. Whether in physical or virtual space, it is clearly possible to project a carefully controlled image or to be authentic. It's possible to make mistakes and to share too much or not enough. It's possible to have everything clean and discrete or to have messy and reflective conversation. It's possible to connect deeply with others, or to keep relationships on the surface. It's possible to use technology to share emotion, questions, and searching and it's possible to use it to disconnect from the moment and feelings we are living. It's possible to hurt and be hurt, and that pain feels just as real online as it does face to face. The issue is not what is real and what is not, the issue is how we choose to use these tools, or how we let them use us.

When we let the tools use us, we end up in the time-sucking-vortex. We've all been there: one moment we're just checking in on a friend's status update, and the next minute it's an hour later and we're not sure what happened, or we're spending so much time trying to stop feeling lonely even with our hundreds of "friends," or worse, we find ourselves doing exactly what the naysayers mock—sharing only what we had for breakfast and what we're wearing today and our struggle to choose the right shoes for the weather. But these are not the only ways to interact with technology!

Some people have insisted that if we want to realign ourselves with regard to technological life, the only way forward is to stop using it and start living "real life" again. We don't think these kinds of drastic measures are required—in part because, well, this *is* real life. Real life is complicated, requires boundaries and self-care, involves different levels of interaction for different contexts, and asks us to navigate an increasingly complex, yet shrinking, world. We won't advocate leaving behind flesh-and-blood relationships, because we believe that living as incarnate beings does require physical experience. We don't want to see everyone in front of a computer or phone screen while oblivious to the people around them. We *do* want to encourage a way of approaching our technological selves with a spiritual lens.

At the most basic level, all of us want to be connected. We crave relationship—to know and be known, to have someone to talk to, celebrate with and confide in. We seek conversation partners who affirm and who challenge. In an increasingly fragmented world we want to belong somewhere, so we create those spaces, building communities of people who share similar interests or use similar platforms. We want to stay connected to those friends and family from whom we have moved away. And we want to be connected to something bigger, which is one of the attractions of the social networks. We know there's more to life than just our own experiences, more than we can really imagine, and one way to connect to that something-bigger is by having ever-larger networks of friends (and even

Facebook "friends") who give us a glimpse of the cosmic reality of which we are a small part.

So, aside from technology fasting (which is good and important occasionally, and we'll discuss it at the end of the chapter), how can we use our vast array of social media as a way to connect to the divine and to the greater world God has placed us in?

One way to start is to be intentional about our community building in those virtual spaces. Being in relationship is more than simply "liking" a status update or broadcasting where you're having lunch (though if you've just discovered a sweet new restaurant and want to post the directions, we're fine with that). Instead of only doing those fly-bys, leave an actual comment. Whenever you log in to one of those social media outlets, make it a point to say something personal to at least one or two people. Start a discussion on your own wall and continue to participate in the thread, making space for thoughtful discourse rather than just "yeah!" or "nuh-uh!" When you see a picture in your news feed, leave a personalized comment rather than just clicking like. Studies show that when we engage in and receive personal feedback, even in online space, we feel more connected and less lonely.[5] Think of it as building community in an asynchronous environment—you can have conversation, encourage people, and offer support even when you aren't in the same place at the same time. The separation of space and time should not necessarily lead to separation of relationship, any more than it did when daily letter writing was a habit families and friends engaged in. Using our social media almost as the 21st century form of pen pals can help us build and strengthen connections. And just as letters were sometimes passed around by family members or read aloud in the drawing room, online groups or communities using the same hashtag can share their lives, get advice, have a space to vent, become prayer groups, and support each other, all through words and pictures on a screen. The fact that more of us live alone than at any other time in history should not stop us from having communities of support, care, and challenge that can reach even into our homes!

> "We lived on farms, then we lived in cities, and now we're going to live on the Internet."
>
> —SEAN PARKER IN THE SOCIAL NETWORK[4]

---

4. *The Social Network*, directed by David Fincher (2010; Columbia Pictures: Columbia Pictures, 2011), DVD.

5. Moira Burke and Robert Kraut, "Social Capital on Facebook: Differentiating Uses and Users", http://mcs.mines.edu/Courses/csci422/PAPERS/p571-burke.pdf.

So next time you see a status update that includes a concern—someone is sick, they posted a picture of their kid's newly-broken leg, a deadline is coming up—take a moment to offer a prayer, even if it's just a one sentence thought sent out into the universe. Then take a second moment to comment on that concern, letting the person know you're holding them in the light and supporting them even from far away. Do the same when you see a celebration—graduation, engagement announcement, new job, whatever it might be. Send some thanks out into the ether, and put those congrats out too. It seems so simple. We rarely think of these networks as prayer lists, though in many ways that's exactly what they are. We put our lives out there, hoping someone will notice and share their own lives with us. We put our hopes and dreams and concerns and failings out there, hoping that someone will be there to offer a virtual hug or a supportive word. It's no different than sharing joys and concerns in the midst of a church service, or writing a letter home sharing our story and asking for advice, except that it's more public and the people who hear it more diverse. When we widen the net of our prayer, and our pray-ers, we can build something entirely new together—something that looks surprisingly like the Kingdom of God.

If you're not in a place where you can or want to put yourself out there or create your own content, one way to engage in the spiritual side of technology is to simply use it as the post-modern version of a devotional. Back in the day, it was common for people to carry around small books that contained scripture, prayers, short essays or meditations, and even artwork. In the middle ages some of these tiny books were filled with hand-painted icons or devotional images that helped illuminate the text and offer a multiple-intelligences approach to seeking God. These are still out there, but most now exist in the form of websites and blogs rather than very expensive pocket-size books. If you're looking for something like that—where you receive and don't have to create, and where you won't be distracted by the comments of others—try a daily online devotional. Some that we like are the short (2 minute) devotions at www.d365.org. They include background music, scripture, a few paragraphs to ponder, a prayer, and a blessing. If you have more time or if you're more an aural than a verbal/visual person, try the podcast from www.pray-as-you-go.org. Each day's is about 12 minutes long and includes music, sacred text, questions to think about, and prayer prompts. You can stream it from the website or download a whole week at a time, load it on your iPod, and take it with you on your commute. Or perhaps you really need something that'll show up in your email inbox every day without you having to remember a website—if that sounds like you, consider the Still Speaking devotional emails from the United Church of Christ.[6] Each morning you'll receive a short scripture text and a story or thought-provoking reflection, along with a brief prayer. These can be great ways to start your day oriented toward the Holy.

If you'd like something that has the potential to be more interactive, consider using blog-reading in this way. There are thousands of blogs offering daily or weekly posts that include words and images to feed your soul, spark your imagination, and prompt new ways of thinking or acting. If the word "devotional" weirds you out, think of it instead as a daily reminder to check in with what God is doing in your life. Find a blogger who matches your style, whether that means mostly words, more pictures, or daily music posts. Follow along as they post their own journey with the Holy, and allow their words to sink in and stimulate your own thinking and praying. If you feel moved, comment along the way too; though that's certainly not required, it might help you feel you are part of a community traveling the same road together. If you have time, perhaps find a couple of options, so that if someone misses a day you still have plenty of material to keep you going. Also, drawing on a variety of spiritual styles will make space for the Spirit to move in new ways—maybe today it's a photo that really caught your heart, while tomorrow it's an inspirational quote or a movie clip and yesterday it was someone's personal story in the comments. Approach this reading just as you would if you were sitting down with a prayer book, and you'll find that the Spirit is moving all over the world and all over the Internet! Not sure where to start? Check out the end of the chapter for a few of our favorites, and then utilize their blogrolls to expand your options!

If you've ever been someone who thought "I should keep a journal," starting your own blog might be for you. A blog doesn't have to be just a chronicle of your days, though you can certainly use it that way. It can be a photo album, a collection of thoughts and experiences, a platform for your opinion, a place to hone your writing skills, or even a way to document your life with God. Some of us find journaling by hand in a beautiful notebook a therapeutic and spiritual experience. Others of us find it an extremely difficult discipline to maintain. With a blog, there's always the possibility that someone will join you in your journey, which both offers some accountability to keep it up and changes the dynamic a bit. Rather than just your private thoughts and feelings, you also have to be aware that nothing on the Internet is ever truly confidential or truly removed. So if you do decide to blog, do it wisely!

6. Check out http://www.ucc.org/feed-your-spirit/, where you can sign up for the daily email and find lots of other resources as well.

A few tips (we know these may seem obvious, but we know people who've gotten into trouble…):

- ❧ *Don't* blog during work hours.
- ❧ *Don't* use people's real names or identifying information if you don't have permission.
- ❧ *Don't* use your blog solely as a place to complain, especially about your work.
- ❧ *Do* tell your own story in your own words, whether you think you're a writer or not.
- ❧ *Do* post pictures, quotes, videos, or links you find intriguing, inspirational, or beautiful.
- ❧ *Do* interact in the comments of your own blog, as this is a great way to get to know new people and build community in a new way.

In a journal, you would likely note important things that happened or things that caught your attention during the day. The moment you caught your breath at the beauty of sunset, laughed at the antics of your pet, or felt tears spring to your eyes. Put these things on your blog, with pictures or video if you can, and allow God to speak through you. You may find you're better able to organize your thoughts in writing, or better able to see patterns of God's movement. You may discover your gifts as you write about things you're passionate about. You may end up in a discussion that opens your mind and spirit to a new way of being. And you may also be a blessing to others who were looking for a little something to fill their cup today, even if you think you can't write or are a terrible photographer, or even if all you're sharing today is how watching *Fraggle Rock* on streaming Netflix makes sick days bearable. Whether your blog focuses on one topic or is a smorgasbord of ideas, photos, food, travel, hopes and dreams, puppies, and book reviews, it can be a way to channel and recognize the Holy in your life.

A blog can allow God to speak through you.

Not ready to put everything out there for the world to see, but still like the idea of journaling online? Try www.750words.com, a website based on the idea of morning pages (from *The Artist's Way* by Julia Cameron). There you can write daily, but only you can see what you write. There's a community there for support and ideas, but no one has access to your writing. Bonus: you get little virtual rewards for every day you write! It can be a place to stream-of-consciousness brain dump, or a place to hone ideas, or a place to just keep track of what you did today. It's completely yours and completely private. Think of it as the computer version of that paper journal, only with fun animal stickers that encourage you to come back and keep up the discipline of daily writing. It also offers some insights on each day's 750 words, such as the mood or tone, whether you're mostly focused on past/present/future, etc. It can be a fascinating practice to look back and see where your spirit has taken you over a particular period, noticing the ups and downs of life and where God was in the midst of all that.

Maybe you aren't really a word person. That's okay too! There are tons of ways for you to engage your faith online without committing to hours of writing or reading. Pinterest offers one way to do that. The basic concept for Pinterest can be found in its name: you "pin" to an online bulletin board pictures and pages you're interested in. Along with boards dedicated to style, sweet rides, work-out motivation, and event planning, you can find collections of inspirations or reflections. Moving images and word art based on motivational quotes can be found all over the web, and now you can create one location to bookmark them all. Having a down day and need a pick me up? Go to your inspiration board and look at images of kittens and puppies hanging out together. Need a reminder on why you work to make the world a better place? Login to see the Martin Luther King, Jr. quote you've pinned that always inspires you. Along with pinning images you find online, you can also search within the Pinterest community by keyword. Type in "hope" and you'll see images and quotes other people have gathered and find meaningful. You can "like" a pin, comment on it, and re-pin the image to your board if you like. In this way you can both create a space for your own faith reflections and share with others on their own journeys.

Perhaps you're one of the people who has another problem: inability to turn *off* the social media. If you hyperventilate at the thought of missing a check-in on Foursquare, if you can't make it through dinner without checking Facebook, or if you're so tethered to your smartphone that your friends wonder if they'll ever see your eyes again, perhaps it's time to try the fast. No, not the faster network. A fast in which you turn off the Internet for a little while. Back in chapter 2 we talked about fasting as a way to refocus and to break the power of those things that so easily enslave us. If you find that your face-to-face relationships suffer or disappear, or even if you just have trouble focusing on the task at hand, it could be good to try a reboot. Maybe you just need an hour or two, or maybe you need a whole day or a weekend. Either way, a program called "Self-Control" may be for you. It's a free downloadable piece of software that allows you to blacklist certain domain names for a specified period of time, up to 24 hours. So if you need your work email, but want to avoid Facebook, Pinterest, and Twitter, you can put those on the blacklist and they will mysteriously be unavailable to you, no matter what you do, until the timer runs out. It seems extreme, but some of us need the help. When you return to the social networks, remember to use them, don't let them use you.

Just as the Internet offers zillions of ways to get information, it also offers myriad ways to look for the movement of God and to connect your spirit with something larger. And just as "real life" can be messy and complicated or shallow and appearance-oriented, so can your life on the Internet. The issue is not whether one way is real and another not—it's all real life. What matters is how we engage and whether we're looking for the divine or only looking for ourselves. If you're willing to be authentic, to look past the surface and engage deeply in the issues and lives around you, and to be on the lookout for a spark of the Holy, life online can be as real as anything else. Don't, of course, use technology to divorce yourself from your physical self or from face-to-face relationships. The best uses of social media empower us to build relationships that continue off-screen, and the best uses of social media connect us to the greater good.

GOING TO PRACTICE

Check out a few of the websites in this chapter and see if any of them tug at your spirit.

Next time you log on to a social media site, take a moment to pray for the people in your newsfeed, and to let them know you're thinking of them. Let it be a space for building up the kingdom of God with encouragement and hope, rather than just another procrastination tool.

SEE MORE

Here are a few blogs your authors enjoy as tools for seeking the Holy in everyday life. Check them out as a springboard for putting together your online devotional life:

Godspace: http://godspace.wordpress.com
The Questing Parson: http://questingparson.typepad.com
Any Day A Beautiful Change: http://kewp.blogspot.com
A Church For Starving Artists: http://achurchforstarvingartists.
    wordpress.com
Posts From an (un)Tamed Cynic: http://johnvest.com/
    john-vest-blog/
The Painted Prayerbook: http://paintedprayerbook.com/

TEN

GOING, ALL ALONG

Some keep the Sabbath going to the church;
I keep it, staying at home,
With a bobolink[1] for a chorister,
And an orchard for a dome.

Some keep the Sabbath in surplice[2];
I just wear my wings,
And instead of tolling the bell for church,
Our little sexton sings.

God preaches, — a noted Clergyman, —
And the sermon is never long;
So instead of getting to heaven at last,
I'm going all along!

—EMILY DICKINSON, 324[3]

woman known for being a recluse reflects so well how the simple sights and sounds of a garden can bring you as close to God as any church service. Though she rarely left her room in her later years, Emily Dickinson appreciated how the world around her spoke of the divine. Ironic, isn't it?

---

1. Bobolink? A blackbird that spends its time in parts of both North and South America. Dickinson included this bird in several of her poems—here it serves as a member of her choir.
2. Yeah, we had to look this one up too. A surplice is a type of vestment (churchy outfit) that's worn by worship leaders in the Roman Catholic and Anglican traditions. It looks a bit like a tunic.
3. Emily Dickinson, *Three Series, Complete*, Project Gutenburg, May 2004, http://www.gutenberg.org/files/12242/12242-h/12242-h.htm, (accessed June 23, 2013).

Emily understood something that preachers and priests across the centuries have often forgotten—God can be found in the world around us. Too often in Western religious traditions, leaders have encouraged their followers to view the world around them as some sort of way station, as though we're here and suffering and dealing with all the crap on earth until we get to that proverbial "better place." If we're to do anything here on earth, it's to dominate and tame this wild and unruly world while we wait for the next one.

Bull. With global warming, loss of green space, pollution, and so much more, we can look and see just how spiritually (and physically and emotionally) damaging this way of viewing the world is. It's not even theologically sound to boot! We are not above and beyond the natural world—we're smack dab in the middle of it. The particles that formed the earth, the sun, the galaxies are the same particles that form us. We're part of that ever-evolving, ever-expanding universe. And that can be mind-blowing. In the grand scheme of the cosmos, we're like little bits of dust. How minuscule we seem! Yet our dust is the same as stardust. How connected we are!

> Our dust is the same as stardust. How connected we are!

The wonder of the universe and our small but still significant place in it hopefully makes you pause. As we are all connected (at the elementary particle level!) to our own world and all of its inhabitants, to the quark and the quasar, we are connected to that which brought it all into being. The universe speaks of the One who kicked off that big bang, who brought creation out of chaos, who made all that is (seen AND unseen) and called it good. By spending time meditating on and mingling with creation, we get to know the Creator.

For some of us, seeing God in creation is as simple as the sun rising in the east. The beauty of a sunset, the majesty of a mountain vista, the power of the tide—our world reaches out and calls us to God. For others of us, the occasional sunset is nice, but getting entangled with vines or closer to critters does not sound like a good time. It's not that we don't love the great outdoors, it's that we love them through windows and clouds of bug spray. After all, there's so much yuck out in the wild world—Allergies! Bugs! Dirt! Excuses (complete with exclamation points) are easy to find. To be fair, many of us come by them honestly.

Between the lack of neighborhood parks, lack of time, distrust of unstructured play, and fear of the outdoors, many of us have grown up separated from natural space. Compared to the generations before us, we're prudes when it comes to intimacy with nature.[4] We experience the natural world via cut flowers at the grocery store, watching the squirrel run around on our back porch, or adding *Shark Week* to our instant queue.

If this sounds like you, then the first step to embracing creation as part of your journey to fully embrace God might be this: step outside. No, really. Just step outside. Once you're outside, go find some green space. This could be your own front lawn (if you've got one), a larger patch of grass at a nearby intersection, even an old lot that's been overgrown with weeds. If you're not too afraid of strangers staring at you, sit down. Yes, in the grass. Let your fingers run through the stalks, notice what you feel. Is this greenery smooth, rough, itchy? Do you notice any little bugs crawling around down there? See any ants carrying food home? What about other little critters who call this patch of land home? Take about 15 minutes to absorb this space with all your senses.[5] Maybe you'll notice nothing profound, or maybe by taking the time to just be in a part of the world you normally walk on by, you'll know a moment of wonder.

> *"I love to think of nature as an unlimited broadcasting station, through which God speaks to us every hour, if we will only tune in."*
> —GEORGE WASHINGTON CARVER

To run with Carver's metaphor, we tune in better once we get rid of any interference. Static of all kinds put up barriers that keep us from truly embracing our connection with creation and from knowing the Center. If we want to connect to God by being connected to creation, then perhaps we should take down some of those barriers. Whether you're a beginner at this nature thing or an old hand, you can always get a little bit closer to the world around you and thus to God.

---

4. In his book *Last Child in the Woods: Saving Our Children from Nature-Deficit Disorder*, Richard Louv offers evidence (much of it anecdotal for our generation) that since the 1950s and 1960s, American children have been spending less and less time with the natural world. This is thanks to lack of time and increased fear of what's out there in the wild unknowns, as well as cultural priorities placed elsewhere. Louv shares the story of a college professor—Jerry Schad—who brings a class out to Mt. Laguna Observatory. Each year, fewer and fewer of his students have seen the Milky Way in its splendor before. Schad says: "most are very impressed with what they see and learn, but for a significant number the trip is downright frightening. Several have mentioned the trees in the forest at dusk in the same sentence as *Blair Witch Project*." Richard Louv, *Last Child in the Woods* (Chapel Hill: Algonquin Books, 2008), 130-131.

5. Feel free to skip taste if that weirds you out!

When was the last time you went camping? We mean really camping. Not roughing it at a hotel without free Wi-Fi, but sleeping bags, tents, campfire, outdoor toilets. If you're not an experienced camper, then pick a site nearby (like a local state park) and one that'll have other campers—perhaps even a few well-versed folks that a novice like you can make friends with! Get into the wild, wonderful yonder where nothing stands between you and creation. No firm roof, no lock on the doors, no microwave, no outlet for all your electronics. Just you, perhaps some friends, and the star-spangled sky.

If you've done the state park, clearly-marked-campsites routine, try something a little more challenging. Get your gear and explore the backcountry. Enjoy an all-day hike and spend the night either in a prepared shelter or in a place where your presence would make a minimal impact.[6] Whatever you've done before, go just a little bit further. Keep pushing on those barriers that keep you from being one with the rest of life in all its diversity. Get closer and closer to your creaturely roots.

When you push back your barriers, you create more room for holy awe. There's nothing quite like sitting by the remnants of a campfire, letting the heat roll off the dying embers and covering you in a blanket of warmth; looking up at the strands of stars that make up the Milky Way; listening as the silence of the night is broken by owls conversing with each other; knowing that you are part of something wonderful and loved by *Someone* wonderful. Being able to call up this feeling of connection to the cosmic story not only strengthens your sense of the divine but it can also get you through on those days you feel lonely or lost.

If sleeping outside and waking up to realize you're covered in dirt and campfire fumes in a place with no running water is *really* not your cup of tea, that's okay too—you and Teri can make reservations at the local bed and breakfast together! A hike in the mountains, an evening campfire at your local county park (make sure you get a permit!), an afternoon splashing your feet in the local creek, or a day walking barefoot on the beach can also be ways to connect to nature. The big thing is that you get out into God's great creation and recognize yourself as part of that created order, part of the vast expanse, a piece of a puzzle we can barely comprehend but that will always be a mystery to us if we only look at it through the window.

BARING IT ALL...OR AT LEAST YOUR FEET

Imagine this: a brisk night, a full moon, a receding tide, and three twenty-somethings running down the empty beach toward the water—not even a

---

6. Embrace the pack-it-in-pack-it-out mantra. Whatever you take in to wilderness areas, take back out. That way your fellow hikers/campers (and other creatures) can enjoy the same pristine sites you did.

pair of boxers between them. These young adults dipped their bare flesh in the bitterly cold water, not on some dare and with no thanks to an alcohol-induced "great idea!" The skinny-dipping trio dropped trou and splashed into the Sea of the Hebrides in an attempt to get as close to the natural world as possible.[7]

Baring all in nature is a primal experience. You are as unsheltered and unprotected from the elements as you possibly can be. You're showing off your body to God, the world, and everybody. Wait, maybe not everybody.[8] Without so much as a stitch on, whether you're taking a dip in the lake or sunbathing in a private spot, you can literally feel what it is to be one with the world. You have removed everything—your house, your car, even your clothes—that can trick you into believing you're somehow separate from the rest of the world. You are as physically connected with creation as you can be. Shockingly intimate. In that intimacy, notice not only the physical sensations but the soul ones as well. *Are you terrified, nervous? Exhilarated, free? Do you feel more alive? More united with That Which Is Greater?*

> By removing some—or all—physical barriers we set up between ourselves and the rest of creation, perhaps we can remove some of the spiritual barriers as well.

If you're not quite ready to take such a plunge, try a smaller step. Literally. Go barefoot. In the grass. In the mud. On the smooth flower beds. On the crunchy pine needles. Pay attention to what it feels like—cool, soft, ouch! With each step let yourself be connected, rooted even, in the earth. As you take each step, open your other senses to the world around you. Notice that the air may smell different. Listen for sounds you don't normally hear inside. Lift your face up to the sun and take a deep breath. Maybe even close your eyes and let your other senses do the work, connecting to the world in a different way. By removing some—or all—physical barriers we set up between ourselves and the rest of creation, perhaps we can remove some of the spiritual barriers as well.

---

7. Don't worry, no toes were lost to frostbite.
8. If you take up this particular practice, note that it is *not* an invitation to exhibitionism. Make sure that before you get naked, you get safe. Safe as in no one is going to accuse you of public indecency and no one you're uncomfortable with is going to see you in your birthday suit.

WAIT, WHAT? THERE'S HOMEWORK REQUIRED?

There is only so much of the world you can see from your house, from a car, from the sidewalks of your town. The windswept plains, the mountain vistas, the warm beaches, the mysterious caves—from the bounteous to the barren, God is there. For some of us, every moment we're outside, we see God. We stand in awe of the commonplace pine tree, with its tight spiral of branches and prickly cones. Every single sunset is a miracle. Others of us no longer see the trees, nor do we take time to appreciate the colors that paint the sky. We've lost our sense of wonder. How do we get it back?

One of the easiest ways to get your wonder back (or increase it) is to bone up on your natural history. You're out on a hike and walk past an old rock fault. You notice a thrust of rock at a 45° angle. Thanks to the ten minutes you spent online looking up the geological history of the area you're hiking, you know that you're seeing evidence of the continental collision when Pangaea formed. Wow. Right there in front of you, the history of that supercontinent! Here you are, millions of years later, walking right by. You and the collision of continents, together. Pretty awesome. And something you might have missed out on had you not known just a bit of the history of the area.

The geology of the world isn't the only thing that can bring on the wonder. Remember that list of excuses that keep some of us away from the world outside? Snakes, spiders, and poison ivy are among the "DANGER: KEEP OUT" signs. Heeding only those signs, you risk missing out on the small yet stunning elements of our world. For example, if you don't know which spiders in your area are poisonous, you could hurry past a beautiful—and harmless—arachnid. If you don't know about the flora and the fauna that you should stay away from, you might just think you need to give wide berth to something that could move you rather than hurt you.

Something can happen when you spend time out there—in the woods, in the desert, in a cave, in the sea. When you, as a creature, engage creation, you open yourself up to the mystery of the Creator. The more you know, as the NBC slogan goes, the further you'll go. Or, perhaps for our purposes, the further into the mystery of the divine you'll fall. When you're out in God's world and open to the mystery while you're there, the earth may speak. You see a creek, snaking its way through a small valley. Turning the corner, you see the creek has been covered with a small avalanche of rocks. How sad, you think. The creek's simple path has been blocked by those rocks. Except, as you keep walking you notice that the creek actually keeps flowing. And that ability for something as clean and simple as water to find a way, even with such obstacles, speaks to you as if a message from the heavens.

Opening yourself up to the wonder of the world around you, allowing yourself to embrace what God may be trying to say through the trees and the fields, the mountains and the vales, you may be delightfully surprised how deeply you feel the presence of the Maker of All Things.

If you do experience such a profound moment, if you are blessed to know a place where God seems to break into the mundane world and show you a feast of wonder, hold on to that! Hold on to the feelings and the memory and the trigger. No really, *hold* on to it. If you're walking along the beach and feel the Spirit's breath in the ocean wind, pick up a seashell that you can later touch and recall this moment. If you're hiking along the mountain path and see the most beautiful change in leaves, the majesty of God's paintbrush laid out before you, bend down and take a fallen leaf to press between the pages of a book. If you're standing by a brook, listening to angels sing in the bubbling of the water, hold onto a pebble from that stream so that you might have a literal touchstone.

If you're lucky enough to know several sacred places in the world, keep a divine drawer! Place your mementos from the world in one location so when you need to be reminded of God's presence, you can go to this treasure trove. Or arrange these holy trinkets around your space—your home, your work, even your car—so that everywhere you are, you might find a reminder of the magic you once felt.

Please don't take anything from the wild that still has a place in its habitat. What does that mean? Well, flower picking is out. So is disturbing the natural landscape. If you do take a memento, you should make sure you're not doing any harm to the environment or the beauty of the place by doing so. Which is why pictures are one of the best ways to hold onto the memory of a divine moment. Sure, with a photo you don't get the tactile or olfactory sensations, but you can be assured that you didn't negatively affect a sacred space when taking it. Keep a photo journal of your sacred places—of the creatures you saw that moved you, the landscapes that touched your soul, the wonders of the world that made you gasp in awe.

Part of the wonder of the world is that we can't carry it around in our pockets. Be open to keeping mementos, yes, but also try the opposite. Dare to just live in the moment and let it pass, no memento, no picture. That sunset that moves your spirit is only to be experienced in this moment, in this place. Be completely and totally present in this created space and time, and let the beauty of the Creator dwell in you rather than rushing to find a way to memorialize it.

While you're reconnecting with your creaturely roots, don't forget there are lots of opportunities to do some good while you're out there. Our planet is at risk, and it's mostly our fault. So, in addition to not littering yourself, pick up trash when you see it. Use your feet instead of a car as often as you can. Build community and save the planet at the same time by carpooling to work or taking public transportation. Get to know a local farmer at a farmer's market and learn about issues of food sustainability, and take a few minutes to educate others the next time you serve local carrots instead of baby carrots from the grocery store. They may be small steps, but whenever you do them, you remember you're part of a bigger whole, one piece of a big puzzle, one beloved child amidst the beloved creation. When we conserve and buy local and recycle, when we clean up the ground and air and water, we are connecting to the One who created everything, called it good, and made us stewards—caretakers—of this whole beautiful place.

THE WHOLE WIDE WORLD... FROM A SAFE DISTANCE

We would be remiss if we didn't add that while getting *out* into the world is delightfully soul-filling, you don't necessarily have to leave your living room to engage the wonders of the nature world. Panda-cam, anyone? No, seriously. It's one of Teri's favorite things. Different zoos, wildlife centers, and animal rehabilitation centers have webcams dedicated to their most precious (and often precocious) residents. You can spend hours watching the antics of a baby elephant play in the mud, a wounded owl learn to fly again, an endangered polar bear splash around in water.

While the more exotic animals can certainly inspire the soul, let's not forget the domestic variety. Many of us already know the beauty of having a pet—someone to greet you when you come home, to love you unconditionally—there's not much in the world that compares to the soul-filling experience of a dog excited to see you even when you've been gone only a couple of hours, or a cat snuggling up on your lap to purr the evening away. There's something holy about this connection between humans and beloved animals. It reminds us that we don't only have relationships with other people, but with many other parts of God's creation, and that we are not the only ones with the capacity to love. Does a dog love the way a spouse does? Well, okay, probably not (because that would be weird!) but in some ways, the unconditional love of a pet is a better mirror of God's love for the world than our own oft-conditional love is. This connection between us and another part of the natural world helps take us out of ourselves and come in tune with God's vision of the peaceable kingdom, where the wolf and the lamb, the lion and the kid, the child and the scorpion, all lay down together. Not that we're advocating having scorpions for pets.

Living in the fertile Shenandoah Valley, I (Amy) can't escape the local food movement. Farmers' Markets and farmer friends means yummy fresh, local foods abound. And these foods tempt. Tempt persons who had sworn for years they had a black thumb (that'd be me) into believing they too could grow plants aplenty in order to enjoy delightful salads and veggies.

One day in the late spring, my then-boyfriend (now husband) and I started growing a container garden. We lovingly planted tomato, peppers, squash, peas, broccoli, spinach, and basil. Throughout the spring and beginning of summer, Dave and I watered, weeded, and watched. Buds, blossoms, and then the beginnings of beautiful fruits formed. I watched from my kitchen window as tomatoes grew, until they were just about ready to harvest. And then I looked out that same window one morning to see nothing—nothing but stubs of plants where once, delicious fruit grew. Our friendly neighborhood groundhog had had himself a tasty midnight snack.

Peppers grew and then… groundhog. Squash… groundhog. Peas… okay, you can guess where this is going. Hundreds of dollars and many hours of gardening later, Dave and I harvested a few basil leaves. The groundhog feasted gloriously that summer while we had none. This is my experience with gardening. When I don't kill something, another something gets to enjoy my efforts.

Still, this was a significant spiritual experience. I had heard gardening was supposed to be a holy thing. After all, the Christian scriptures begin and end in a garden. Yet every time I've tried to be all holy and prayerful while digging in the dirt, all I could think was "where's my freaking moment of Zen?!" It's never been particularly peaceful. But this container garden was different. Things actually grew. I got excited. And then… Dave and I put in the work but saw no harvest. It stinks. Really stinks. But it's part of how our world works; we only have so much control. We can't affect all the variables. Groundhogs are gonna do what groundhogs are gonna do.

Where's my freaking moment of zen?

Putting all that work in and coming out with nothing (at least in the food category) is incredibly frustrating. It's also surprisingly refreshing. No matter how many books we read or how much planning we do, our world continues to surprise us. We can only control so much, plan and prepare so much, and then we just have to live. The container garden was an exercise in risk—a spiritual practice anyone living in our economic times should appreciate. We risked, and we failed, and yet we somehow learned, gained.

Even if what we grew didn't come to us, we were still a part of creation and *another* part of creation ate lots of delicious veggies. And somehow, that experience spoke to me about *the* Creator and *the* creation. Some look at our sacred creation stories, note how we are made in the image of God, and think, "hey, it's all ours!" These folks tell the tale of power and dominion over creation. The story of our failed garden tells me another tale. Dave and I had our own plans for the plants we nurtured; the groundhog had another. Had we ultimate power, were we the ultimate creators, we'd have been feasting on home-grown veggies all summer. We may have responsibility for the earth, but not dominion. No matter how much we might like to imagine ourselves as top of the food chain and in charge of the world, we are still made of material things. We are still part of the creation; not the creator. Our task is not to subdue and use, but to join the rest of creation in praising the One who feeds the groundhog with daily vegetables even as we pray for our daily bread.

Seeing the raw beauty around us is one of the most moving things in our human experience. Looking, touching, hearing the natural world can be powerful reminders of our place in the universe, and can spark our imaginations as we ponder what other wonders the universe might have in store. It's no wonder people often say that their spirituality is rooted in their experience of nature. Tuning in to the show that creation is putting on is one way to connect with the Creator, and to let that creative energy flow through us as well. Be playful, be observant, risk some dirt, and see what divine beauty is calling you today.

GOING TO PRACTICE

It's a beautiful day. The sun is shining, the temperature is perfect, and you've got work to do. If it's an option for you, take your work outside! Grab your laptop, your textbook, your papers to grade, and go find a sunny patch. Unable to leave the workplace? Use one of those 15-minute breaks to just step out and get a few minutes of fresh air, and remember that when you breathe, you can pray. Try to make a commitment to going outside when the weather is wonderful, no matter how much you have on your plate.

SEE MORE...

Jamie S. Korngold, *God in the Wilderness: Rediscovering the Spirituality of the Great Outdoors with the Adventure Rabbi* (New York: Doubleday, 2008).

ELEVEN

THE HOLY IN THE MUNDANE

"To think we must abandon conversation with God in order to deal with the world is erroneous."

—BROTHER LAWRENCE[1]

n February 2012, a photo-montage meme known as "what I really do" had its fifteen seconds of internet fame. Every profession, nationality, pastime, and animal seems to have been the subject of one of these charts, consisting of a black background and a set of six photographs, laid out in a 3x2 grid. Starting with the top left, the usual progression was: What My Friends Think I Do; What My Mom Thinks I Do; What Society Thinks I Do; What My Boss Thinks I Do; What I Think I Do; What I Really Do.[2]

While many of these were amusing and many more were so esoteric as to be nothing more than Facebook-clutter, they almost all share something in common: the disparity between the last two boxes (What I Think I Do and What I Really Do). Add in the fact that the last picture on many of these grids is of a person falling asleep/tearing their hair out/looking in despair—all on a pile of books or an overwhelming stack of papers—and we have a startling and sad realization that many of us believe that the life of our imagination is more worthwhile than the life we are living.

It may be true that life is less interesting than we imagined, especially for young adults, and especially when we find ourselves in work environments

---

1. Brother Lawrence, *The Practice of the Presence of God* (New Kensington, PA: Whitaker House, 1982), 12.

2. http://knowyourmeme.com/memeswhat-people-think-i-do-what-i-really-do

that don't live up to the intellectually, socially, and economically stimulating jobs we dreamed of. But even if our lives do seem to be consumed with never-ending piles of seemingly pointless paperwork, it is still possible for us to find a connection to something greater. Sure, we may have imagined that we'd be out changing the world, finding deep meaning and joy in feeding the hungry, creating peace on earth, or saving future generations, and that stack of file folders and overflowing inbox doesn't feel like it's anything but meaningless stress. Don't throw in the towel yet! It doesn't mean that deep meaning and joy have left the building.

Looking for and experiencing the Holy in the midst of the mundane tasks that make up everyday life is an important practice. Sometimes life is exciting and the tasks we do are so obviously holy moments, but most of life is the day-to-day stuff we do because it's what makes up, well, life. We cook and clean, commute, do a job that (no matter how awesome) sometimes has boring parts, we watch TV or read, we pay bills and answer emails. So how can we transform our to-do lists into Holy opportunities?

The seventeenth-century monk Brother Lawrence suggests the first step:

*"We should offer our work to God before we begin,
and thank God afterward for the privilege of having done it."*[3]

That seems easy enough. Whenever we begin a task—whatever the task may be—we can offer it up. The point here is not what kind of words we use to make this offering, whether we speak aloud or silently, or even necessarily the name of the One we address. This exercise is about awareness, intention, and a willing spirit. It is about knowing that what we do is only one part of a whole so much greater that we cannot even see the full picture. It is about knowing that whether we do great things or small things, we can do everything with great love. (Thanks, Mother Teresa, for that inspiration!) So the next time you begin a task, even if it is as mundane as sharpening pencils or making copies, offer it up to the Holy One before you begin, and when you are finished, spend a moment giving thanks for the privilege of having done it.

Now, of course some tasks don't feel like much of a privilege. Whether it's cleaning the cat's litter box or gutting a flood-ruined house, grading a stack of mediocre multiple-choice tests or re-organizing the racks at the store for the umpteenth time in a shift, there are some things we have to do that are just unpleasant. It doesn't feel like a privilege to fold the

---

3. Brother Lawrence, *The Practice of the Presence of God,* 23.

same four stacks of t-shirts every fifteen minutes just because people rifle through them unthinkingly. It doesn't feel like a privilege to smile while taking away someone's plate of "not-what-I-ordered." But is there something in even the most unpleasant of tasks that we can offer up, something we can be grateful for, something we can find even a smidge holy? Even if it's as simple as the privilege of being physically and mentally able to do a job, or the privilege of playing a part in the lives of young people even if the multiple-choice test is the most boring thing ever to grade. These are things for which we can give thanks. Without these privileges, we would not be able to do the task before us. Even cleaning the litter box has hidden joys—the joy of cat companionship and the joy of knowing they're using the litter box instead of the furniture! And, of course, often if we dig deeper, we can find privileges far beyond these surface thanksgivings. We may tire of people saying "well, at least I have a job" or any of its variations, but there's something there. Amy has to do dishes sans dishwasher (first world problems, we know). She's taken to thinking about the blessing of clean, running water every time she scrubs a pan. What are the deeper joys and privileges of your mundane tasks?

Both Brother Lawrence and Mother Teresa talk about doing everything—no matter how small the task—for the love of God. If we love God in and through everything that we do, then no matter how gross or how menial, the things we do are holy and purposeful. Having a sense of this purpose can transform the way we approach everyday life. Suddenly it's no longer just the overwhelming stack of papers sliding off the desk as we lay our heads down in defeat. Instead even that stack of papers becomes an opportunity to love in small and unknown ways.

You know how Grandma's cookies always taste better? Or Mom's meatloaf, or Dad's scrambled eggs? That cliché about the secret ingredient being love may not be so far off. Could it be that when we truly pay attention to what we're doing, and do each small thing with great love, it really does result in better cookies, better relationships, better lives? Most of our grandparents, and many of our parents, didn't have the opportunity to truly multitask the way we do now. When Teri makes a dinner that takes lots of preparation, she often listens to podcasts or talks on the phone while she chops and stirs. Her grandmother, though, just stands at the counter and chops and stirs. For many of us (Amy excluded), washing dishes means giving them

> "We can do no great things; only small things with great love."
> —MOTHER TERESA OF CALCUTTA

a cursory rinse and finagling them into the dishwasher. Tidying up the house or organizing the office is an opportunity to listen to interviews or TED talks. Working out is the perfect time to catch up on the shows languishing in the DVR. Rarely do we do just one thing, and truly be in the moment of that thing. More often, we're trying to do several things, or even to actively take our mind off the tedium of the thing we're doing. Sure, the same workout video for the 57th time is boring—unless you're also laughing along to last night's *Daily Show*. Chopping vegetables or washing dishes is made so much more entertaining with "Stuff You Missed In History Class" podcasts.

But what would happen if we did even those boring everyday things with great love? Not necessarily love for those activities, but a bigger-picture kind of love, the kind that seeks connection, meaning, and transformation. What would happen if we turned off the TV and the iTunes and the phone and simply chopped, simply washed—simply *paid attention* to the things we are doing with our bodies? Is there something of the Holy to be discovered in these small things? Or are they really just throwaway activities we need to get out of the way in order to find the Holy in the next thing?

Thich Nhat Hanh, Buddhist writer and teacher, thinks there's more to life than always taking our mind off what we're doing now. He teaches about mindfulness—learning to be in the moment in order to truly live the amazing life we've been given. In *The Miracle of Mindfulness* he says:

> While washing the dishes one should only be washing dishes, which means that while washing the dishes one should be completely aware of the fact that one is washing the dishes. At first glance, that might seem a little silly: why put so much stress on a simple thing? But that's precisely the point. The fact that I am standing there and washing these bowls is a wondrous reality. I'm being completely myself, following my breath, conscious of my presence, and conscious of my thoughts and actions. There is no way I can be tossed around mindlessly like a bottle slapped here and there on the waves.

> If while washing the dishes, we think only of the cup of tea that awaits us, thus hurrying to get the dishes out of the way as if they were a nuisance, then we are not "washing the dishes to wash the dishes." What's more, we are not alive during the time we are washing the dishes. In fact we are completely incapable of realizing the miracle of life while standing at the sink. If we can't wash the dishes, the chances are we won't be able to drink our tea either. While drinking the cup of tea, we will only be

thinking of other things, barely aware of the cup in our hands. Thus we are sucked away into the future—and we are incapable of actually living in a minute of life.[4]

We don't know about you, but the idea of missing life, incapable of living even as it passes us by, is an even more frightening prospect than the realization that the great things we dreamed we'd spend our lives accomplishing may not be our immediate reality.

> "Folding sheets like folding hands,
> to pray as only laundry can."
> —CARRIE NEWCOMER[5]

Chores generally seem so tedious—that's why they're called "chores" after all. It's hard to imagine that a life made up of these mundane moments is worth paying attention to, and yet they are a part of the one wild and precious life we have been gifted.

Take Brother Lawrence's advice, and when you begin a chore, take a moment to dedicate the work you do as an offering to God. Cleaning the bathroom or vacuuming the bedrooms can be an offering of love—love for your partner or housemate if you have one, love for yourself (you deserve a clean space!), love for creation, love for God who has gifted you with this home and with the responsibility to care for it. No matter how small the thing, if it is an offering of love, it can be great. These moments can also be times of sensing God's love for you—you are participating with God in the ordering of an environment, in the creating of an atmosphere. Try to be conscious of God's love flowing through your breath as you do these small things, and soon you may find that your whole space has a bit of an aura of grace.

When you pay your bills, whether you do that through your bank's website, through writing and mailing a check, or with an app on your phone, take a moment to give thanks for the resources you have been gifted, and to remember those who do not have the resources for things we often take for granted. Even if you're looking at your bank balance and the bills and wondering how this can possibly work out, remember you are not alone. It is entirely likely that your peers are silently struggling

---

4. Thich Nhat Han, *The Miracle of Mindfulness* (Boston: Beacon Press, 1975), 3-5.
5. Carrie Newcomer, "Holy As the Day Is Spent," *Gathering of Spirits,* Philo (now Rounder) Records, 2002.

alongside you. It is also entirely likely that those who struggle less in this area may be praying for you as they pay their own bills every month! As we try to be good managers of what we've been given, it sometimes feels like such a burden to simply figure out how to make ends meet, and looking at the online banking screen can cause a mild panic attack. Take a deep breath and be honest about what those numbers tell you. And be honest about where your money goes. Remember that a look at your bank/credit card statement will tell you more about your real priorities than anything you say—where you spend your money and your time are often the things that really matter. Do the numbers reflect your priorities? Do they paint a picture of you that you want to display? If so, rejoice! If not, ask the Spirit to lead you in painting a different picture. Can you find a way to give to a good cause, whether it's your church or your local homeless shelter or the food bank or even your local NPR station, as a part of your financial stewardship? Remember that money isn't really ours any more than life itself is—it's a tool we're given to use in making the world a better place. Be sure some of your money is going to make the world a better place.[6]

Each small thing we do, each task in which we are mindful while we perform it, adds up to a life. The question is: will our lives be great by virtue of our having lived them fully, or will we miss them entirely? We are a generation that believes we can change the world—and we can. As David LaMotte says in his WorldChanging101 workshop, "it's not naive to think you can change the world, it's naive to think you can possibly be in the world and *not* change it." The question is *how* we will change the world.

The first step toward being a positive influence on the world is to recognize that each of our small things is part of the Big Thing that God is doing in the world. If God is love, as we believe, then everything God does is done in love. Even the divine equivalent of doing the dishes. We aren't God but we can seek to emulate doing all things in love. We can seek that greater sense of purpose and being. Connecting to the reality beyond our normal perception will require paying attention to what God is doing in every moment. It will require not abandoning our conversation with God in order to deal with the world, and also not abandoning the world in order to deal with God—instead we need to learn to keep up our conversation with God *as* we deal with the world. Theologian Karl Barth asked preachers to keep the Bible in one hand and the newspaper in the other. We don't think that should be limited to preachers, or to the newspaper.

---

6. See the "what, no lambs?" section of chapter 12 for more ideas on using your money for the building of the kingdom of God.

We bring the world with us into our relationship with God—and God does the same.

COMMUTING WITH GOD

One place we can work on this practice is on our commute. Many of us travel some distance—whether it's a ten-minute drive, an hour-long train ride, or a fifteen-minute walk—to get to work or school each day. All of us travel at some point, for shopping, visiting, or just running errands. Many of us go nearly on auto-pilot, paying little attention to our surroundings beyond what's necessary for basic safety. Commuting is the perfect time to commune with the Holy in our everyday space. What better time to keep up our ongoing conversation with God than on this tedious commute?

Next time you get in the car, try something radical: turn off the radio. Use the time, whether it's a few minutes or an hour, to enjoy the silence. Notice the thoughts that run through your head, notice the colors passing by your window, listen to the sounds of the road or of nature or even of your car. Where is God in this quiet space and time? In silence we're able to both speak and listen, yet thanks in part to all our favorite devices and the wonderful distraction they provide, there's not much silence in our world anymore. So grab it when you can. Being alone in a car, in the quiet, can be a peaceful oasis in the midst of a busy world. Sure, commuting has a purpose—you're going somewhere—but can you just *be* in that moment? Just be driving, just be looking, just be listening. Perhaps that morning and evening drive can become a time of setting the tone for the day, a time of focusing on what matters. Some people use that commuting time to separate work and home life, making the car a transitional space where frustration can be transformed into grace. One way to do that is to drive in silence, offering the time and space to God.

If you do have the radio on, take the opportunity to pray about the things you hear. Hourly newsbreaks are like endless prayer request lists. Even traffic reports can be cause for prayers for help or of thanks! Interviews are opportunities to listen for the movement of the Spirit in the life of another person. And, of course, the music on the radio, even if it's the top 40, can be part of your spiritual practice as well! Notice when lyrics draw your attention, or when a melody makes you want to sing along. What is it about that song that connects with your spirit? Does the song speak to your emotional state, to the reality of your life, to your hopes and dreams? Is there a song that summarizes your experience of God or your adventure of faith? Can you use the songs on the radio to hear the movement of the Spirit, or to express your own feelings to God? Of course sometimes the songs on the radio are not exactly great theological treatises. But there's often something that can spark your imagination—a word or a phrase, an image or a snippet of melody. If you hold on to that and let the rest of the song be a backdrop for the thoughts sparked by that one little thing (as long as you're still paying attention to the road, of course) the radio can be a great way to pray your way through your commute. Intrigued by how you might pray along with the radio? Check out chapter 4 for more on that.

Many of us were taught that when we see an emergency vehicle, especially an ambulance or a fire truck, we should not only pull over to the side of the road to let them pass quickly and safely, but we should also offer a prayer or send out some good vibes to the people involved in the emergency. Don't forget the emergency workers too—EMTs, firefighters, drivers, and dispatchers. They need our prayers and our positive energy as they work to save lives and property each day. When you're driving to work or school or to the grocery store, if you see flashing lights or hear a siren, turn off the radio and take a moment to offer those people and their situation up to God, sending some hope and healing energy their way. Sure, they may cause traffic jams or inconvenience us as we try to pull over across three lanes, but that inconvenience can also be an opportunity for us to practice compassion for neighbors we do not know.

> "I run for the bus, dear,
> While riding
> I think of us, dear,
> I say a little prayer for you."
> —DIONNE WARWICK[7]

If your commute is via public transportation or carpooling, and you usually take your iPod along with you, try a prayer podcast. One of our favorites is from pray-as-you-go.org. It combines music, scripture, meditative questions, and prayer for a 12-15 minute prayer experience. Something like that is a great way to center your day. You can also try the practice of commuting in silence—if you usually have your iPod with you on the train or bus, try keeping it in your bag for a few days and really noticing all the sounds and sights around you instead. As you look at the other people commuting with you, try to see the image of God in them. As you hear the conversations those annoying people in the next

---

7. Dionne Warwick, vocal performance of "I Say a Little Prayer," by Burt Bachrach and Hal David, originally released from *Windows on the World* album (Scepter, 1967).

row are having, listen for the movement of the Spirit in their lives. As you see the landscape or the city rushing by the window, take a moment to notice something beautiful. God is already around you and within you—and others, even the annoyingly loud people—so use this time to try to see and hear with new eyes. Remember that, as Teresa of Avila said, "Christ has no body on earth now but yours," which means that when you see, God sees. Can you see and hear with God's eyes and ears? How might that change your perspective on the world and the people around you?

SPIRIT-LENSES

At the end of a day filled with random or frustrating moments, you'll probably be looking for a way to relax. Lots of us like to relax with TV or movies, and these too can be a place where you can look for what God is up to, and where your eyes can be the eyes of Christ seeing the world. It just requires putting on your Spirit-lenses. Just as 3D glasses help us to see the way a film's creators' intended us to see, Spirit-lenses can help us see the way the Creator intended. Try watching TV and asking yourself where you catch a glimpse of something holy in the show. Where are relationships life-giving and grace-filled? Where are people experiencing God in their midst? How is the creation showing glory? What other spiritual stories (from scripture, from other books, or from your own life) are being played out? Many television series and many movies explore themes of brokenness and redemption, of light and dark, of struggle and triumph. Are there other themes or storylines or moments that catch your heart's attention? Sit with those and wonder, let your imagination run, and ask yourself what the Spirit might be saying to you through that story. We know that God is all about stories, and that good stories are often about the intersection between ourselves and something bigger than we are. Find yourself in the story, and ask yourself how it illustrates the bigger story God is writing. Learning to engage various media with Spirit-lenses on is an important skill if we're truly going to experience God's presence in every moment.

We can use those Spirit-lenses wherever we are—not just with movies but with the news, with encounters with our neighbors, with our officemates, with the checkout clerk, with the person who has a full cart in the express lane, with the people driving alongside us in traffic. We can choose to be on the lookout for grace, almost like investigators. We're out sleuthing for good news, for glimpses of God's big story. We may find those glimpses in our email inbox, or in putting the recycling out on the curb, or in traffic, or in the clean laundry that still needs to be folded.

When we're purposefully and mindfully looking, we begin to see our world as God-infused, and our tasks as sacraments and prayers. And that new perspective is exactly what we're going to need if we're going to seek God—who is often hidden in plain sight, if only we would open our eyes to see how holy the mundane can be.

GOING TO PRACTICE

Pick a chore, any chore. Preferably one that comes up more than once in a while. Now try that mindfulness thing with this particular duty. Take note (or literally, notes if you want) of how you felt being fully present while performing that chore. Keep track of your feelings/reflections over a period of time—a week, a month. Do you notice anything different about how you feel toward that chore? About yourself? About life?

SEE MORE...

Thich Nhat Hanh, *Peace Is Every Breath* (New York: HarperOne, 2011).

TWELVE

~

TAKING IT TO THE STREETS

"I am in the world to change the world."
—KÄTHE KOLLWITZ

D o you want to make the world, your nation, your local community a more equitable and just place for all to live? We're betting you do, and based on statistics that's probably a good bet. Older generations have bemoaned the fact that people in our age range have pulled away from what is considered traditional civic engagement. Statistically, we don't read newspapers (though you have to wonder if Internet news counts in those surveys), we don't join unions, we don't do club meetings, and we don't affiliate with formal civic groups.[1] Despite the efforts of *Rock the Vote* and other movements encouraging young adults to get out and vote, the numbers of young people who turn out still aren't stellar (even with a slight uptick in the last decade).

No, things don't look like they used to. What older adults have known as the norm wasn't always the norm either. The infrastructure of the civic realm is shifting again, and young adults are pioneers in the new ways of engaging civic life. So it's true that we generally don't want to join the Rotary Club or Junior League, and no, we won't volunteer to serve on the board of even the most worthy civic organization for the next four years. But you know what we will do? Show up and swing a hammer. Make a meal for someone who's homebound. Fundraise for a cause we care about. Because for many of us, doing good in the world really is a wonderful way to get to know who we are, find our purpose, and connect with God.

---

1. Richard Settersten and Barbara E. Ray, *Not Quite Adults* (New York: Bantam Books Trade Paperbacks, 2010), 45.

Giving of ourselves and serving others is often the first place we feel a connection with the Holy One. We may not be able to explain why; we just know there's a tug at our hearts that happens when we put others before ourselves occasionally. Perhaps we're just living into the truth of Jesus' words: "just as you did it to one of the least of these who are members of my family, you did it to me" (Mt. 25:40).

Be it a tug at our hearts or an intentional living into the words of Jesus, we young adults have become increasingly fond of volunteering—giving time and talent for efforts that better our world. Some would like to throw a caveat in there: volunteering can be almost anything with any variable of time and talent committed, from helping a little old lady cross the road to spending a year in the Peace Corps[2]—as though that broad definition lessens the impact and importance of this increased involvement. We think the diversity of volunteering enhances the possibilities for making meaning in our time. Want to make a difference? You have all the options in the world. Now, go do something.

Okay, so it's not quite as easy as that. When it comes to opportunities to serve, there are a lot of options. Which is fantastic—and overwhelming. You might feel a little like I (Teri) did on my return home after a year living in a poor neighborhood in Egypt. In Cairo, my little local grocery only carried one breakfast cereal: Corn Flakes. So for a year, I pretty much ate Corn Flakes. My first day back in the US involved a "quick trip" to the grocery store, where I encountered an entire 40-foot aisle of cereal choices where there used to be only half an aisle. When I left for Egypt, there were four flavors of Cheerios, and a year later there were eight, and every brand had undergone similar expansion. Surveying the overwhelming number of options, I felt my breath get shallower and my vision narrow, until finally I saw the familiar rooster and walked out with yet another box of Corn Flakes.

The world has many needs, and there are so many ways you can help that we understand if you grab onto the first opportunity that arises (or even just stay at home). The tyranny of choice is as real in our volunteer options as in our consumer choices. Before you end up either frantic or frustrated, remember that while one person can make a world of difference, one person isn't responsible for making all the difference in the world. In the midst of so many good causes, our vision can narrow and we can forget that this choice is not the one that will make or break society.

Those of us who are prone to carrying the weight of the world on our shoulders ought to remember what Paul said: "Now there are varieties of

---

2. Peter Levine, *The Future of Democracy: Developing the Next Generation of American Citizens* (Lebanon, NY: University Press of New England, 2007), 84.

gifts, but the same Spirit; and there are varieties of services, but the same Lord; and there are varieties of activities, but it is the same God who activates all of them in everyone. To each is given the manifestation of the Spirit for the common good" (1 Cor. 12: 4–7). In other words, there's more than enough good work to go around and, even if it doesn't always feel like it, more than enough hands and hearts to do this work. The kingdom of God (by which we mean times and places where God's will is done and all are treated like the children of God that they are) breaks through all around the world all the time. Want to be a part of that amazing experience? You don't need to save the world; you just need to find the place where your gifts can be put to good use.

YES, YOU CAN

We've watched (and participated in) the protests against wars in Iraq and Afghanistan, lived through the campaign and election of Barack Obama, experienced the demands for change in the Occupy movement; we're hard-pressed to suggest our generation hasn't experienced any meaningful participation in our world. Many of us have found a particular cause or movement and thrown ourselves in head first. By giving time and talent, we found something that matters. In those discoveries of things that have meaning, we connect to our fellow human beings, to creation, to the Source of goodness and hope.

Not all of us have found our calling in movements against Wall Street or for a politician. Some of us are still searching for the cause that will be *ours*. It's okay if you have no idea where to even begin thinking about where you'd like to serve, or if you've just begun to suspect what your particular passion may be. In order to find a volunteer opportunity that holds deep meaning for you, that reveals to you great (or small) truths about yourself or life or God, it helps if you find a spark that sets fire to your passion for service. Are you concerned about people sleeping out in the cold or heat tonight? A first step toward a better world might be donating socks or blankets to a local shelter, or offering to help serve a meal. There you might meet someone or hear a story that leads you to become a regular midnight volunteer, or passionate about advocating for affordable housing, adult education, or access to mental health care. Each small step can lead to many different paths toward becoming a builder of God's good world.

If you feel the urge to commit to something but don't know how to choose what to do (there are so many problems to address, after all), here's a helpful discernment process borrowed from *Stick Your Neck Out:*

A Street-Smart Guide to Creating Change in Your Community and Beyond by John Graham.

First, look around. See what's going on in your community. What are the needs that aren't being met? If you don't know, ask around. Ask your civic and religious leaders where they see the greatest needs and what might be done. See too what's going on in your larger community. What are the issues of justice that might be addressed on a national level? What about global? What are the greater needs in our world that you might be called to address?

Once you've learned about the needs of your community (be it local, national, or global), think about what makes you particularly passionate. When you hear a news report about the lack of access to good medical care in certain areas, do you feel that fire of injustice burning? When you talk about solutions to big issues like malaria being simple—if only people would just pay attention and care—does your heart rate increase? What makes you want to learn more, talk more, do more?

What makes you want to learn more, talk more, do more?

Reflect also on what you know, what you're good at, and what you've had experience with. Think about the different times you've volunteered for something or gotten passionate about an issue. Is there a theme? Graham suggests even making a volunteer résumé as if you were applying for a job. Read through it as a potential employer or headhunter. What area of service would you invite yourself to do?[3]

Finally, make sure your decision isn't based solely in logic. Discerning where your spirit will flourish in service doesn't mean only looking at what you're good at or have done before or what you know the most about. It's also about what feels right. Calling is about what the divine desires for you. For those who are not intuition-based decision makers, this may be harder than for others. For all of us, discerning what God is asking us to do in this world demands deep thought and prayer. We can all benefit from the wisdom of good friends. Invite your intuitive friends and/or those who seem to have an ear for God's voice to help you navigate those gut feelings, the tugs on your heart, the still small voice of God.

You may also try this exercise we picked up from our good friends at Bread for the World (a non-partisan advocacy movement aimed at ending

---

3. John Graham, *Stick Your Neck Out: A Street-Smart Guide to Creating Change In Your Community And Beyond* (San Francisco: Berrett-Koehler Publishers, 2005), 4.

hunger). Take a sheet and make two columns. In the first column, list the things you know people are already doing in your community to address the needs of whatever area or cause you're drawn to. What immediate actions are people already taking that you might get involved with? For example, if you think you'd like to work with issues of hunger like the folks at Bread for the World, you might list working at food pantries and soup kitchens, sorting cans for the Salvation Army, and collecting nonperishables for the food bank. In the second column, write down causes of the issue at hand that you'd like to address. Again, say you're interested in hunger issues. Why is there an imbalance of resources? Why are people chronically hungry? What are the root causes? Now look at both columns. How do they relate? Where might God be calling you to both serve hands-on and to advocate for systemic change?

Once you've found a place, a cause, or a people you wish to serve, don't let your discernment stop there. It's sad but true that people with the best intentions can often do more harm than good. We see someone in pain and immediately want to reach out and make that pain go away. That instinct is good (and helps distinguish us from psychopaths). But when we reach out, we ought to do the best we humanly can to make sure our help is actually helpful. Sticking with the hunger theme, let's think about food aid. You see pictures of starving children in, say, Ethiopia, and immediately you want to give them food. So you call and write to your senator and representative to increase the nation's food aid budget for that area. And, miracle of miracles, it works! Your voice is heard and more food is being sent over so those hungry little bellies will be filled. All is good, right?

Maybe not. Setting aside corruption and theft, the food aid program itself may be contributing to the cycle of poverty and hunger. Many of the nations where hunger is rife actually produce (or have the capacity to produce) enough food to feed all their people. The problem is cost and distribution. When a developed nation comes in and gives away free food, usually sent over from its own fields and farms, it undercuts local farmers and food. With the addition of foreign food (as opposed to foreign money to help purchase local food), food stability and self-reliance becomes an even more distant goal to reach.

Does this mean you should just sit back and watch children go hungry, either across the globe or across the street? Of course not. But if you are to offer your time and heart and talent to others as part of your continuing journey with God, make the effort to educate yourself on what impact you may or may not be making. God's dream for the world is not contained within our personal warm fuzzies. Serving is not about making ourselves feel good (though that's not a bad side effect). So beware of letting feeling good about oneself trump offering what people actually need. Whatever you do, whether it's joining an already established program or forging your own volunteer path, be diligent in making sure your service is meaningful to you *and* helpful to others.

WE CAN CHANGE THE WORLD, WITH OUR OWN TWO HANDS

For those of you who grew up watching things like the Miss America pageant, picking out a "cause" may make you feel a little too much like a beauty pageant contestant with your pet platform. Some of us do thrive with one major focus, something we can get involved in and make as much of a part of our lives as we want, whether for a month, a year, or even many years. With the time we put in and the relationships we build with other activists and volunteers, we feel like we've come to know a bit of the kingdom. Others of us find one cause too limiting. We'd rather explore all the possibilities for service and advocacy. It's not that we have volunteer ADD (okay, maybe some of us do), but rather the more we know about the world and its needs, the more we need to help. No, we can't solve all the world's problems, but we can give a little of ourselves to many different places and people. The little things matter. We never know what seeds we may be planting—seeds of equity, of justice, of hope. Yes, the world is full of big problems, but we dare to think that one small act here and there matters too.

Being open to opportunities that pop up involves being aware. We don't just mean keeping an eye out for flyers or calls for volunteers on Craigslist (though those are good). Pay attention to your local news. If you live in a small town, consider subscribing to the paper. As in getting the actual newspaper delivered to your doorstep. We know, we know: we just talked about how our generation doesn't do newspapers and that's completely okay. But if you live in a small town or in a neighborhood with its own news source, that source is a great way to be connected.[4] If you're feeling particularly daring, you might also look into your town council minutes. Yes, they'll probably serve as a good substitute to a sleeping pill, but they'll also be a gold mine of information about your community. Sometimes the most pressing issues aren't the ones that get popular coverage. Be proactive in discerning the key issues and what might be done in response to need, and you've just opened yourself up to a variety of opportunities to serve.

---

4. Yes, many small-town newspapers have online options but in our experience, they don't always have the best design and webmasters. Besides, when it comes to local news, you may not always know the headlines you'll want to click on for further info. Go ahead, be a little quaint and subscribe to your local paper. Consider it helping your local economy.

When you've learned about your local community—whether you're now a frequent visitor to town hall meetings or you've just got some idea of the non-profits in your area—get involved hands-on. If you're a member of a faith community, that can be a great starting point for service. Does your church or synagogue serve regularly at a food pantry or Meals on Wheels? Does your spiritual home recruit volunteers to drive the elderly to doctors' appointments or to run errands for the homebound? If there are activities you want to get involved in, but you can't because of the timing (e.g. you work during the day, so can't serve lunch at the Tuesday soup kitchen), talk to the leaders of your church, synagogue, or mosque. Remind them that retired folk and stay-at-home parents aren't the only ones with time and heart to give, and work together to create volunteer opportunities during non-business hours.

You certainly don't need a community in order to volunteer locally, but it does help. If you're interested in joining established service opportunities but don't have a faith community of your own, you can look to civic organizations, or you can always scour the websites of religious communities and see if you can tag along without being a member. You can also nurture your own community with an emphasis on service. Get together with friends and volunteer to walk dogs at your local SPCA. Challenge each other to see who can raise the most money for the next Relay For Life event. Volunteering does not require a community, but having one as you seek to serve can make giving back a richer experience.

As you think about giving of your time and energy, consider taking a volunteer vacation. Mission trips with faith communities and alternative spring breaks are popular versions of these types of vacations: traveling not to soak up the sun and see great sights, but to serve and give of yourself. In your travels you meet new people and experience a different way of living, even as you seek to offer your talents and your heart. There are plenty of opportunities all over the world and with almost any kind of non-profit you can imagine. You can go for a week or even a few months. Yes, joining in with a church or college group would make planning such a trip easier, but it isn't necessary. Either alone or with friends, check the travel section of your local library or bookstore. Just as there are guides to eco-traveling and foodie holidays, there are guides to volunteer vacations.

Be forewarned: if you take a volunteer vacation, you may never be the same.

Seven years ago this is what I (Amy) knew about Ethiopia: good coffee and Lucy the fossilized hominid can be found there. I wasn't wrong about those things—during my three week mission trip in the country I saw Lucy and drank more than my fair share of delicious coffee. I also discovered how much I didn't know—how much I couldn't know—just from reading fact books or talking to others who had been there. It was three weeks of traveling across country, worshipping, eating, working, laughing. Three weeks and my life can never be the same.

I can never look at a sweet child running up to me at church and not imagine the children I met across that impoverished country. Children who welcomed me with big smiles and bigger hearts.

I can never drink a Sprite without thinking about Brano, my driver and friend who made sure I had a constant supply of the soda when my stomach was upset.

I can never see corn on the cob and not recall the kindness Tujube showed our group. This strong, smart woman, the first ordained female leader in her church, shared her stories, her wisdom, and her delicious roasted corn, all of which she generously offered.

I can never hear the stories of people in other places and other lands, people who struggle each day to survive, people who do not have easy access to medicine, clean water, or education without thinking about my friends.

I can never hear one of my favorite passages of scripture— "There is no longer Jew or Greek, there is no longer slave or free, there is no longer male and female; for all of you are one in Christ Jesus" (Gal. 3:28)—without lifting up in prayer the people I met and the friends I made.

I cannot unlearn the stories of those I met; I can never forget the needs and dreams of my sisters and brothers across the ocean.

I can never be the same.

I don't want to be.

WHEN MONEY TALKS

We may wish it weren't so, but let's face it: money talks. What we do with our money and where we choose to spend our funds matters. So here's the good part: our money can help us find meaning. Not in a "let-me-buy-my-way-into-enlightenment-and-bliss" sort of way, of course. Rather, as we make informed choices and spend with care we may find it's possible that that which has been called the root of all evil can actually do some good. And that right there, the ability to take something as basic as spending and create a positive change, is a step toward a whole life focused on justice and compassion.

As with many of the practices in this chapter, faithful spending is going to take a little research. The organic food movement has proven that people are willing to spend a little more if they think it is healthier for them. Why not spend a little more time and/or money to make sure the products you buy are good for the people who made them? A few minutes is all it takes to check on producers of clothing, household items, food. Yes, you may love those new shoes you bought at a great price, but if the price is so great because of slave labor, maybe those shoes aren't so sweet after all. Instead, find out what standard goods you buy are available in fair trade options. Rather than buying a pound of coffee from a corporation that underpays their employees in developing nations, buy a pound of fair trade coffee so you'll know that those who picked and processed the beans are being paid a fair wage. You can also get fair trade clothes and handicrafts (which places like Ten Thousand Villages have made popular), sugar, tea, honey, wine, fruit, chocolate, and even flowers. That sounds like the makings of a romantic—and just—night.

> "When money talks I hate to listen but lately it's been screaming in my ear."
> —BEN FOLDS[5]

Being faithful with your money isn't limited to day to day purchases. If you are one of the few young adults who have begun to invest for the future, consider looking into ethical investing. While saving for retirement is great, ask yourself if you're okay if your dividends come from investing in ethically dubious corporations.

We aren't under any delusions: avoiding, even straight up boycotting, certain products or companies is not an easy task. About a decade ago there was a boycott on Taco Bell that was supported by many different faith groups. The Bell purchases tomatoes from farms in and around Immokalee, Florida, a farming community that utilizes immigrant workers for their picking process. These immigrants worked in sub-standard conditions and hadn't seen a raise in over 30 years. They were asking for increased wages (a penny per pound of tomatoes picked) and better working conditions. Taco Bell (and its parent company Yum Brands, Inc.—home of Pizza Hut, KFC, and more) would not negotiate. And then came a boycott. For those of you who do not drool over the thought of a Crunchwrap Supreme, the sorrow of driving past a Taco Bell may not register for you. But it did for both of us, and for many of our classmates. In fact, at that time, Taco Bell was the only place a vegetarian (like Teri) could get a fast food meal. So believe us, every time we did drive by (or worse, drive through with friends who weren't

---

5. Ben Folds Five, performance of "Emaline," by Ben Folds and Evan Olsen, on *Ben Folds Live* album (Sony, 2002).

boycotting and had to say "no" when they asked us if we wanted anything), it was a challenge to hold onto our convictions. But it was also, we believe, the right thing to do. And a few years later, when Taco Bell finally agreed to the workers' requests, you better believe there was a huge caravan from Columbia Theological Seminary (where we both went to graduate school) running South of the Border. We enjoyed both a burrito and the satisfaction of knowing some small good had been done.

Here's a fair warning: once you know, you can never un-know. What do we mean by that? You may not want to become informed on *every* company's less-than-ethical practices. It's just too much. It is the rare person who can go from blissful ignorance to informed spending in every aspect of life. Starting your practice of faithful spending is going to be challenging enough without being overwhelmed by all the concerns in the world. We suggest starting at one point: one fair trade product to buy, one product or company to avoid. Start somewhere and let the Spirit guide you from there. Once you've got a handle on your first step, take another, and little by little, go deeper and deeper into the world of faithful spending.

WHAT, NO LAMBS?

When it comes to our money, it's not just how we spend that can make a difference. By giving of our resources, as well as our time, we get to be a part of little kingdom moments. Okay, some of us have jobs that already feel like volunteer work, and some of us are scraping to get by. With student loans and credit card debt, it's hard to imagine writing a huge check to your church or clicking the Paypal button on a large donation to Doctors Without Borders. That's why tithing is one of the hardest parts of being part of a faith community. What's tithing, you ask? Going back to the time of Moses, tithing was a complex system wherein people set aside one-tenth of crops, cattle, and other resources for those who had little or none. Nowadays it's a general catch-all phrase for giving to a faith community, though many still hold up the 10 percent as the biblical model. It's one thing when you've got a lot of money and 10 percent means a smaller vacation house, and a whole other thing when 10 percent means saying goodbye to any safety net against bouncing checks. You've got to decide what you can give.

Ignatius of Loyola dreamed of giving without thinking of the cost. We dream of giving while being fully aware of the cost. Knowing what you're giving up in order to give to others reminds us all that money is not what life is about. It also reminds us that no matter what the culture around us may preach, we don't have resources for the sole purpose of making our own lives better. What we possess we use not just for our own benefit but for the benefit of the world around us. Psalm 24 reminds us that "the earth is the Lord's, and everything in it," and the story of Abraham and Sarah gives us an example of being "blessed to be a blessing." When we think of our resources as a gift that God has entrusted to our care, for the purpose of blessing others, it changes our view of money and time and even of the talents we so carefully cultivate. We learn to see with the eyes of the One who offers us these gifts, rather than our own often self-serving lenses.

When we look at our resources in this way, searching for ways to be a blessing to others, we find that going past the comfortable, stretching a little, is good. Sacrificial giving reminds us what really matters in this world. What would it look like if you gave enough that you could no longer afford something simple like name-brand peanut butter? Would you appreciate what you have even more? Would you realize how truly rich you are? Would you feel more connected to people in need around the world thanks to your giving?

If figuring out a budget and being disciplined enough to stick to such a number is just beyond your capabilities at the moment, don't fret. There are other ways to give sacrificially. For example, do you stop by your local coffee shop on the way to work for a cup of joe? Then for a week, don't. Instead, calculate how much you'd spend on coffee that week and give it to Nothing But Nets, a campaign that seeks to protect people from malaria by purchasing, delivering, and educating families on malaria nets—all for 10 bucks a net. A week with no coffee may be hard, but think of what your sacrifice means for a person a continent away: life. When put in that light, giving up coffee for a week may seem like a small sacrifice, but don't discount it: it still has meaning for you and it definitely makes a difference for someone else.

The phrase "the gift that keeps on giving" is an old advertising slogan that's been around since at least the 1920s, when it was used to promote phonographs (aka talking machines). Today the best example of that slogan we can think of isn't the phonograph's great-great-great grandchild, the iPod, but a Kiva card. Kiva is an organization based on microfinance wherein you can "loan money to the indigent, those without collateral, career changers, and those without any work experience."[6] Loans are made at reasonable rates to folks an average bank wouldn't go near.

Instead of giving someone in need a handout, you can support someone's dream and their plan for a better life. In this way you offer them the

6. Josh Clarke, "How Microlending Works," *How Stuff Works*, April 29, 2012. http://www.howstuffworks.com/microlending.htm.

double blessing of help when they need it and the gift of knowing their hard work pays off. You can give loans to help a Kenyan single mother rent farmland in order to grow and sell tea; you can help a Mongolian husband and father support his family by loaning money to build a workshop; you can help a group of Mexican craftsmen and women purchase supplies they need to make furniture.[7] Microfinance has enabled people across the world to make a better life for themselves and their families. Perhaps that's why Mohammad Yunus, founder of the microlending Grameen bank, won the Nobel Peace Prize in 2006.

Kiva collaborates with microfinance institutions around the world so that entrepreneurs on five continents can benefit from the power of the Internet. Since 2005, Kiva.org has made it possible for people to visit the website, read the personal stories of loan-seekers, and then give to those whose situations they find the most compelling. You can fund from $25 up to the entire asking amount if you so choose. Once the entrepreneur has the money she or he needs, she or he goes to work, and you get periodic updates on how her or his project is progressing. These updates are perfect for praying over, too. Every entrepreneur can use a little divine light to work by, after all. Little by little, the loan gets paid back (and it does get paid back, as the minuscule 1.09% default rate in 2011 highlights).[8] As the borrower pays back their loan, you are repaid and can either re-lend your funds, donate it to Kiva for their operating expenses, or withdraw it. See? It really *is* the gift that keeps on giving, a blessing that multiplies! So, when someone asks you want you want for your birthday, consider saying "a Kiva card!"

> *"The Spirit of the Lord is upon us, because she has*
> *anointed us to bring good news to the poor.*
> *She has sent us to proclaim release to the captives*
> *and recovery of sight to the blind,*
> *to let the oppressed go free,*
> *to proclaim the year of the Lord's favor."*
> —PARAPHRASE OF LUKE 4:18-19

The words above are the same words Jesus used to inaugurate his earthly ministry, altered to include us all. Because we *are* included. Whenever we volunteer our time and give of ourselves for those in need, we are of the

---

7. All of these examples were taken directly from the Kiva website, www.kiva.org, May 12, 2012.
8. *Kiva Annual Report 2011*, accessed May 11, 2012, http://annualreport.kiva.org/#letter.

same Spirit as was upon this man from Nazareth. Whenever you seek to know God through service, you open yourself up to the power of that Spirit. So whatever you do, be it build houses or give blood, text money to disaster relief or travel across the world to build a well, when you give of yourself, your time, your talent, and your resources, do so with an open heart. Allow yourself to be surprised at what God is doing through you. You may volunteer to be a child advocate in order to help a kid, only to discover you're sharing love and care with a whole family. You may think you're going somewhere to help someone else, only to find you're the one being helped. When you work toward the kingdom of God, when you seek justice and equality in micro and macro ways, when you offer compassion and care, when you give so wholly of yourself, the world really can change. And you, too, right along with it.

GOING TO PRACTICE
Be inspired by the Dorothy Days, the Martin Luther King Juniors, the Mahatma Gandhis, the Mother Teresas, the Oscar Romeros, and the Desmond Tutus of the world. These people sought after the kingdom of God their whole lives long and their stories spark courage and conviction in others. So go to your local library and check out a biography on one or more of these modern day saints.

SEE MORE...
Julie Clawson, *Everyday Justice: The Global Impact Of Our Daily Choices* (Downers Grove: Intervarsity Press, 2009).

A BLESSING

Be careful what you say and to whom you say it.

Not long after we had been ordained and entered into life as young pastors, we found ourselves together again with a former professor. We had "graduated" to being leaders at a conference with her, a rather momentous event for two women who had only a couple of years before been students hanging on her every word. Now she was listening to us as we shared fellowship and frustrations.

One of the frustrations we shared was the lack of published material addressing the reality of young adults seeking sacred connections in the world today. Sure, there were books talking *about* us, and some wonderful memoirs *by* members of our generation. "Why," we opined, "isn't there anything that draws on our experience to offer ideas for integrating the holy into our lives?"

Our esteemed professor and friend, to whom this book is dedicated, looked at us (with *that* look) and said simply "write it."

That was the beginning of our journey writing this book.

Now you've come to the end (or perhaps skipped to the end a la *The Princess Bride!*).

We hope that along the way, whether you've read every chapter or skimmed for highlights, you've found something that resonated with you. A practice or two to try, a new way to look at an old habit, a possibility of connecting to the One who makes all things new.

We hope too that you've found something to be excited about, be empowered by. A chapter, a thought, a practice that inspires you to go out and continue the conversation with friends.

When you put this book down, we hope you go forward reminded that you're not alone in your yearning to connect, your longing for something more.

Go, incorporating the identity of mystery chaser into your life.

Seek the sacred.

Play. Pray.

Pursue the Spirit at work in our world.

The Young Clergy Women Project

is a network of the youngest ordained clergy
women, defined as those under forty. With
more than 650 members, we live across the
United States and around the world, and
represent more than two dozen denominations.
We gather whenever we can—regionally, at
denominational events, at an annual retreat,
and online. TYCWP publishes new, fresh and
evocative articles written by members of our
community on Fidelia's Sisters, and we have
partnered with Chalice Press to publish a book
series authored by TYCWP members.

We do all this to provide members with new
professional and personal relationships and
opportunities to share their wisdom with their
peers.

Learn more about The Young Clergy Women
Project online at youngclergywomen.org.

the young
clergy
women
project

www.youngclergywomen.org

Additional books from *Chalice Press* and *The Young Clergy Women Project*

Sabbath in the Suburbs

A Family's Experiment with Holy Time
by MaryAnn McKibben Dana

Sabbath-keeping seems quaint in our 24/7, twenty-first–century world. But the Sabbath isn't just one of the Ten Commandments; it is a delight that can transform the other six days of the week. Join one family's quest to take Sabbath to heart and change their frenetic way of living by keeping a Sabbath day each week for one year. With lively and compelling prose, MaryAnn McKibben Dana documents their experiment with holy time as a guide for families of all shapes and sizes. Tips are included in each chapter to help make your own Sabbath experiment successful.

• 9780827235212

Named a "Must-Read for Ministry in 2013" by Ministry Matters

Sabbath Supplementals

Group studies and congregation-wide projects will be easier than ever with these new resources that take Sabbath thinking deeper and help readers claim Sabbath time in a 24/7 world.

• Written devotions, prayers and other opening activities to help kick off group meetings
• A complete retreat plan that can be adapted for the needs and interests of your group or congregation
• A series of short videos that will complement the ideas in the book

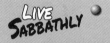

Enhance your journey with our Sabbath water bottle, mug, T-shirt, and "to-do/to don't" post-it notes.

Visit sabbathinthesuburbs.com for more information.

Additional books from *Chalice Press*
and *The Young Clergy Women Project*

Bless Her Heart

Life as a Young Clergy Woman
by Ashley-Anne Masters and Stacy Smith

Humorous essays describe the real-life experiences of young women clergy in this reflection on the everyday realities of pastoral ministry for the young, female professional.

• 9780827202764

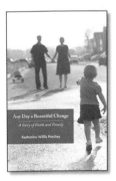

Any Day a Beautiful Change

A Story of Faith and Family
by Katherine Willis Pershey

In this collection of interrelated personal essays, Pershey chronicles her life as a young pastor, mother, and wife with reflective stories that will strike a chord with anyone who has ever rocked a newborn, loved an alcoholic, prayed for the redemption of a troubled relationship, or groped in the dark for the living God.

• 9780827200296

Making Paper Cranes

Toward an Asian American Feminist Theology
by Mihee Kim-Kort

Describing an emerging life and community within North American Christianity, *Making Paper Cranes* engages the social histories, literary texts, and narratives of Asian American women. This book also explores theological projects of prominent Asian American feminist theologians using a liberative theological voice.

• 9780827223752

www.chalicepress.com • 1-800-366-3383 **CHALICE** PRESS

ABOUT THE AUTHORS

Amy   Teri

Teri Peterson is a Presbyterian pastor in the suburbs
of Chicago with a master of divinity degree from
Columbia Theological Seminary. She cofounded and
contributes to Liturgy Link, as well as her own blog,
CleverTitleHere, and is a contributing author to the
Abingdon Creative Preaching Annual 2014 and 2015.

Amy Fetterman is associate pastor at Covenant
Presbyterian Church in Staunton, Virginia. She is
currently working on her doctor of ministry degree at
Drew University.

3/17